THE BETTER ANGELS

The Springfield Years of
Abraham and Mary Todd Lincoln and Their Sons

By Walter Oleksy

Walter Oleksy
Glenview, Illinois

waltmax69@gmail.com

This and my other most recent books can be ordered best at CreateSpace eStore

Dedication

To the memories of Abraham Lincoln,
Mariah Vance, Adah Sutton, and
Lloyd Ostendorf, and that their voices
long be heard.

The cover photograph
of Abraham and Mary Todd Lincoln and their sons

Robert Lincoln is standing, center
Willie Lincoln is seated, front
Tad Lincoln is standing next to Abraham Lincoln

Contents

Introduction – 5
Mariah Meets the Lincoln's – 9
Mariah Vance – 14
Robert Lincoln Meets Billie Vance – 16
Abraham Lincoln – 23
A Hair-Raising Adventure – 32
Mary Todd Lincoln – 35
The Fishing Party – 40
Eddie Lincoln – 46
Something to Crow About – 48
Robert Lincoln -- 56
Willie Lincoln Is Born – 63
Pranks of Willie and Tad -- 69
The Circus Comes to Town – 85
Goats, Ponies, and a Turkey -- 89
Right and Wrong – 95
Abe Comes to Billie's Defense – 100
The Last Time Mariah and Billie
        Saw Abe Lincoln – 103
Death of Willie Lincoln – 110
Tad Lincoln – 120
Robert Visits Mariah, 1877 or 1900 – 126
Abe Lincoln, Children and Pets – 128
Ghosts and Spirits of Abe and Willie – 142
Funny Lincoln -- 153
        Unusual Facts, Funny Quotes,
        Funny Stories Abe Told
Epilogue -- 176

Introduction

A lot is known about Abraham Lincoln, the Sixteenth President of the United States, and some is known about his three sons. Very little is known, however, about their lives together with Mrs. Mary Todd Lincoln in Springfield, Illinois when their sons were boys, before Abe became President and the family moved to Washington, D.C.

A large part of what this book tells about the home life of the Lincolns and their sons in Springfield is based on the recollections of a black woman, Mariah Vance, who was laundress and housekeeper in their home there for the ten years when Abe was a country lawyer until he was elected President. The three Lincoln sons grew up in those years, from 1850 to 1860.

A book by Ruth Painter Randall, *Lincoln's Sons*, was published in 1955 in which she told of Abe and Mary and their boys in Springfield and the White House, but she never knew Mariah Vance's memoirs existed, so she could not include any of her recollections of the Lincoln's. She did, however, learn from other sources and wrote that Robert Lincoln visited Mrs. Vance in Danville in 1900, so she confirms the chapter about that in my book.

We learn from Mrs. Vance that the Lincoln's were a typical dysfunctional American family with their ups and downs, their good times and bad. Sometimes there was strife in the Lincoln's home lives, but also there often was laughter, provided mostly by their two youngest sons.

I wrote about Mariah Vance's life with the Lincoln's in Springfield in a book with Lloyd Ostendorf called *Lincoln's Unknown Private Life*, published by Hastings House in 1995. Some Lincoln scholars said they believed it all, while others doubted parts of it. Many called the book historic for its new information about the Lincoln's. I am writing this book with the caveat that they can believe all of it, part of it, or none of it. I, however, believe all of it, as did Mr. Ostendorf, a major artist of Lincoln portraits who since then is deceased.

In deference to the Lincoln community that did not believe some of the more controversial things Mrs. Vance said in her recollections, I have left them out of this book. This book is mainly to tell about Abe and his boys, and most of that is fun.

The background about this book and my previous book about the Lincoln's and Mariah Vance is that she told her recollections of them and their sons over the years, but no one wrote them down until 1900. Mrs. Vance was then in her mid-80s, doing the laundry each wash day in Danville, Illinois, for a teenage white girl, Adah Sutton, who lived near her. Miss Sutton took notes about what Mrs. Vance told her and years later wrote them up as a book manuscript.

Ostendorf met Miss Sutton and bought the manuscript. I then helped him get it published as *Lincoln's Unknown Private Life*. You can read the complete book in copies still in print or in libraries across the United States,

Now, on with the lives of Abe and Mary Lincoln and their sons in Springfield.

Get ready to laugh a little and maybe cry a little. Believe it or not. There is proof in my earlier book that Mariah Vance lived and was the Lincolns' housekeeper those ten eventful years in Springfield, and that she was loved by Abe and Mary and their sons.

Mariah Vance was a great lady, but history still does not give her any place at all in Lincoln history, much less the high place she deserves. Hopefully, this book will help to achieve that for her and for Adah Sutton, both of them now long gone.

Walter Oleksy
Glenview, Illinois, September 2015

Important Dates

Abraham Lincoln
February 12, 1809 – April 15, 1865
Mary Todd Lincoln
December 13, 1818 – July 6, 1882
Robert Lincoln
August 1, 1843 – July 26, 1926
Edward "Eddie" Lincoln
March 10, 1846 - February 1, 1850
William "Willie" Lincoln
December 21, 1850 – February 20, 1862
Thomas "Tad" Lincoln
April 4, 1853 – July 15, 1871
Mariah Vance
1819 – December 23, 1904
William "Billie" Vance
1842 – January 16, 1904

Mariah Meets the Lincolns

A heavy rain had just stopped on an afternoon in April, 1850. Mariah Vance and her husband Henry went out on the porch of their shack in Springfield with their children and looked up at a rainbow.

She was telling their children about Noah and the Flood, when a tall, thin man in a black suit and tall black hat approached their front yard, having come there in his horse-drawn buggy. They recognized Abe Lincoln because both she and Henry had worked for him. Abe had earlier hired Henry to do some manual labor and Mariah to clean his law office in Springfield prior to moving into it. They liked the lanky young lawyer because he was always friendly to everyone, including black people like themselves.

Abe said hello and then asked how much Mariah charged for doing laundry at his home. He said he was going to be away for a month or perhaps even two, defending clients in law suits in courts in various towns, and his wife needed help with the laundry and their son Robert, who was then seven years old. Mrs. Lincoln was still recovering emotionally from the loss of their second son, Eddie, who had died of tuberculosis two months earlier, in February when he was not yet four years old.

Said Abe: "I know with a very sick woman to work for, it's going to be a trial. But if you'll try to understand my missus, I think you'll learn to like her. And I think she'll like you. Sometimes it's all in getting acquainted. I'm not a saint. I know I have ways which sometimes jar on Mrs. Lincoln."

Mariah listened patiently, glad at the prospect of some work. She did the laundry for some other families in town.

"Whatever you've been earning," said Abe, "I'll be glad to pay you more, because you'll have more trials than at most other places."

Mariah replied, "Since my Henry ain't working now and won't need the mule and cart, he can stay with the older chillums. If he says so, I can take the two wee ones. If you have a place to tuck 'em in, while I works."

Abe said, "I'll be much obliged, and I'll find a place for the children."

He gave the children some stick candy and told Henry he had some work for him at his house later. He told Mariah he would have the water pumped from the well and the boiler on early in the morning for her to start doing his family's washing.

The Lincoln's house was about eight or ten blocks away from the Vance's shack. It still stands today at 426 S. Seventh street, a National Historic Site maintained by the U.S. National Park Service and open to the public daily, containing much of the furnishings the Lincoln's lived with. It is a two-story frame house whose color has variously been described as brown or "a most beautiful dirty clay." A plate on the front door read "A. Lincoln." A fence with gate was out front and the Lincoln boys were said to have enjoyed swinging on the gate.

On the first floor was a family sitting room, formal parlor that was only used for special occasions, and a kitchen. Later, Mrs. Lincoln had the kitchen made smaller to accommodate a dining room.

Mariah arrived at the Lincoln home at seven o'clock the next morning with her two youngest daughters, Julia, 3, and Phoebe, 4, and found Abe stoking wood into the boiler in his back yard.

"The lid of that old battered boiler was bouncing up and down like it had a hot-foot," Mariah recalled. "The wood wash tub with a new-fangled washboard in it was on a stool, and plenty of lye soap. The wash was all in a pile on the floor of a shed.

"I tucked my sleeping younguns in the corner of that shed and asked Mistah Abe if he done had his breakfast. He say, 'All I care for. But there's a mess in the kitchen I fear I can't tackle.'"

Mariah put off doing the laundry and went inside the Lincoln home to the kitchen. There was a big fireplace, a large table, a small work table, and a corner cupboard. Dirty dishes, pans, and scraps of food lay about. She decided to clean it all up before starting the laundry.

She heard a boy come downstairs from the bedrooms. It was Robert, the Lincoln's eldest son, seven years old.

"I never set eyes on such a somber-looking boy," said Mariah. "Proud-looking, too, he was. He had one slightly crossed eye. I loved that little man Robert right off. He then done smiled such a friendly smile, it washed off that somber-looking proud look right away."

Robert asked, "Hey, aren't I deserving of any breakfast?'"

Mariah said, "Land a goodness, you is 'serving of all the breakfast your little fat belly can hold. I'd cook all day and all night to feed such a dear, sweet little boy-man what he likes best. But don't rub that smile off. That's worth heaps of shining gold!"

Robert laughed and his father introduced him to Mariah, telling him she was his mother's new help. Abe then said he had to go to his law office and would leave her in charge. He explained again that he would be gone a month or more, taking cases as a lawyer in circuit courts in nearby towns. It was called "riding the circuit."

Lincoln left and Mariah cleaned the kitchen, then after more than an hour, went into the shed to do the laundry.

Said Mariah: "I was sorting the clothes when step right inside the door was the most prettiest woman I ever laid eyes on. I say, 'Howdy, Miss.'"

Mrs. Lincoln did not reply. She walked over to where Mariah's two little children were sleeping and jerked the foot the youngest, Julia who woke up frightened, and screamed.

"Get these brats out of here!" Mrs. Lincoln cried.

Mariah was about to oblige her, when Abe came into the shed and explained to his wife. "Mother, this is Mrs. Vance, the lady who is going to do the wash and help in the house while I am away."

Mrs. Lincoln was not happy about the children crying, but left and went back into the house. Abe left the shed, and soon afterward Robert entered, bringing a kitten and a ball. He played with Mariah's children the rest of the morning.

When Mariah finished with the wash, Abe praised her for doing such a good job and paid her fifty cents extra. He asked if she would come once a week to do the laundry and she agreed.

Before leaving, Mariah said, "Mistah Abe went on his knees, held Robert close, and kissed him."

He said goodbye to Mariah and again thanked her. Then he went to the barn and hitched his horse, Buck, to his buggy, then left.

"I pitched in and finished straightening out the house," Mariah recalled. "Set Mastah Robert's dinner on the kitchen table, and sent food up to de Missy, then went to the barn. When I come back with my mule hitched to the cart, out come Mastah Robert carrying Julia and leading Phoebe. Sad-like, he say 'Goodbye,' and trotted back to the barn carrying the kitten. Such a lonesome little tyke he was."

Mariah felt sorry for Robert, saying years later,

"How my heart plumb melted for that poor little lonesome-like boy. He was so good and kind. I told my Gawd right there and then, I'd have to go back to that house if only for that poor little boy's sake."

Mariah Vance

Mariah Vance, an African-American woman, was free-born Mariah Bartlett in Illinois in 1819, the exact date not being known. She was a medium-tall, handsome woman who frequently smoked a corn cob pipe.

The 1838 census reveals that in April, 1838 she was living in Springfield, Illinois and was a founder of the Zion Baptist Church.

She married Henry Vance on January 20, 1842. He had been born in Ohio in 1817 and was an African-American runaway slave when they married. The Vance's became parents of twelve children from 1842 to 1862, one of whom died in childbirth.

Henry was a laborer who worked odd jobs, and Mariah worked for ten years as housekeeper and cook in the home of Abraham and Mary To Lincoln in Springfield, Illinois from April 1850 to November 1860.

In 1850, according to the census of that year, Mariah was 31 years old and Henry was 33. They declared assets of only $75, in real estate. By then the Vance's had five children: William, 8; Ellen, 7; Katherine, 6; Phoebe, 4; and Julia, 3. They lived in what Mariah called a shack near the gas works, a few blocks north and east of the Lincoln's home.

Ten years later, in the 1860 census, Henry declared he had $800 in real estate and $50 in personal property, so their finances had improved a little. There were five more children in the family: Julia Narcissa, 8; Rosa, 5; John, 4; Cornelius, 3; and newborn Walter.

Mariah and her husband and children moved to Danville, Illinois in November 1860 after Abe was elected President of the United States and soon afterward he and

Mary and their children moved to Washington, D.C. and took up residence in the White House.

Mariah Vance died in Danville on December 23, 1904 at the age of 85. She was buried in Spring Hill Cemetery in a plot purchased for her and her family by her favorite Lincoln son, Robert, then a grown businessman in Chicago. Her grave remained unmarked until 1964 when friends of Adah Sutton, the girl for whom she had done laundry in 1900, had a small stone marker placed at her gravesite. Her gravestone reads, "Maid in Abraham Lincoln's Home, 1850-1860."

Miss Sutton came from her home, then in Attica, Indiana, to attend a graveside ceremony. She told of how she had met Mrs. Vance and listened to and recorded her reminiscences of the Lincolns.

Said Miss Sutton: "Had I not taken notes during the period from 1900 to 1904, I could not now recapture completely the many wonderful experiences she related to me of her joys and sorrows while she was a servant in the Abraham Lincoln home in Springfield."

Mariah Vance's biographer, Adah Sutton, died in 1972.

Now more of the story of Abe Lincoln and his sons in Springfield from 1850 to 1860, as reported by Lincoln historians but primarily from the recollections of Mariah Vance, mostly in her own words, modified slightly from her African-American dialect.

Robert Lincoln Meets Billie Vance

A week after starting to work for the Lincoln's, Robert Lincoln came running to Mariah's house, frightened. It was a stormy day with heavy rain, thunder and lightning. Mary Lincoln was always terrified at such storms.

"Ma's real sick," he said. "She asks, can you come see her?"

Robert then saw Mariah's boy, Billie. He was eight, a year older than Robert. They were about the same height, but Robert was stockier.

"They took to each other about as how two monkeys in a coconut tree," Mariah recalled.

She told Robert she would take her mule and cart right away and go to his mother. Then, seeing how Robert and Billie liked each other on-sight, she asked, "Mastah Robert, can I take my Billie along in the cart with us?"

Mariah recalled, "Mastah Robert was so pleasured, he had an attack of the chuckles right off. Right there and then I know my black Billie and that blessed white Mastah Robert was going to be everlasting fast friends."

Henry said he would look after the other children while she went to look after Mrs. Lincoln.

Mariah, Billie, and Robert got in the cart and the mule trod faster than normal. She called the mule Maud. It was spooked by loud claps of thunder as another rain storm was coming.

"The thunder got louder and Maud got faster," said Mariah. "The boys laughed with heaps of spirit. I sure believe Mastah Robert was more joyful than he'd ever been."

They were about halfway to the Lincoln home when some rowdy boys tried to stop Maud.

"They was a pack of white rascals," said Mariah. "You'd never know what that darn fool mule were about to do, until she done it. She pushed right smack through that mob, and did they scamper a spell! Then they got their heads together and give us chase with mud balls and screaming at Robert for being with a black family.

The tormenting boys then grabbed the back of the cart and pulled hard. Billie started to get out of the cart to go after the boys, but Mariah grabbed him by the seat of his pants and pulled him back into the cart. Robert had started to follow Billie, but she stopped him, too. She thought that her boy and Robert were no match for the mean boys, so she urged her mule on harder.

Billie saw his father's long black buggy whip and said, "Mammy, here's Pappy's black snake. Give it to 'em!"

By then, the ruffians were climbing into the back of the cart. Mariah cracked the whip at the boys just as a real loud clap of thunder frightened the mule and it charged on. Then a bolt of lightning crashed near them.

"We all screamed and that mess of rascals done must have thought they was struck by that lightning. I swear a war horse couldn't have catched him. The boys scampered away and troubled us no more."

When they reached Mrs. Lincoln they found her on the sofa in the parlor. Mariah told Robert that she was too ill for her to help, so she said he should fetch the doctor right away.

Before Robert could go for the doctor, Billie looked at Mrs. Lincoln and told his mother: "Mammy, look at her! There ain't no need for the doctor. She's peeping! Her's playing possum. Like Grandpappy's pet possum. Just get that black snake and give her a good wallop and she'll forget it that it's blowin' outside."

Mariah discovered then that Mrs. Lincoln was not ill. She was just afraid of thunder and lightning.

Mrs. Lincoln, hearing Billie say Mariah ought to crack the buggy whip at her, got up quickly off the sofa.

"I've come to protect you, Missy," Mariah said.

Mrs. Lincoln was calmed by Mariah's words and her presence. "It was good of you to leave your home and family and come to me. I shouldn't have asked Robert to go for you."

Mariah asked if she could stay a while and clean up the house, which was again in a bad state. She saw some clothes on the floor and asked if she should put them someplace.

"Mariah," said Mrs. Lincoln, "those are for your girls. I've been making dresses out of my darling Eddie's clothes. I was so sorry I disturbed baby Julia's sleep when you came last week. I do so many wrong things when I have these headaches."

Mariah learned later that the Lincoln's son Eddie, born after Robert, had died a few months earlier at the age of three, reportedly of diphtheria. She thought it was no wonder that the grieving mother had headaches.

"Bless your heart, Missy," said Mariah. "You didn't owe my black younguns any dresses. And they're too flub-dub fancy for poor colored folks."

Mariah could also see that Mrs. Lincoln was with child. She was going to have another baby soon, and that might also have made her out-of-sorts.

Mariah looked at the dresses and thought Mrs. Lincoln had put a lot of "love stitches" in them for her little girls.

Robert and Billie had left the room, but came back soon with two stray kittens.

Robert told his new friend, "Ma don't like cats. You can have the kittens, or you can give them to Phoebe and Julia. Pa, he'd bring home all the cats and dogs and other animals he found on the circuit."

Mariah and Billie laughed, while Mrs. Lincoln shook her head in despair.

Abraham Lincoln loved animals. Stories about his affection for animals are many. They included how he climbed a tree to put a small bird back into its nest, pulled a squealing pig from the mud, and plunged into freezing water to rescue his dog from an ice floe.

He allowed his sons to have all the pets they wished, and the result was a family menagerie of dogs, cats, turtles, white rats, frogs, chicks, even a talking crow. He called his horse in Springfield "Old Robin" or "Old Bob." His first circuit-riding horse was "Old Tom," and he had "Old Buck" from 1850 to 1855.

Mariah said Robert recalled, "One time Pa brought us a white rat. It was in one pocket and a turtle in the other. He had put candy in each pocket for them, but the rat ate a hole in his pocket and was about out when he got home. The turtle snapped at his finger as he took it out of his pocket. It's about the only time I ever heard Pa howl. Afterwards, he laughed about as loud as he howled."

Mariah said, "Billie doubled over and nearly laughed his head off. Then de Missy said to Robert, 'Bobby, go up to your room and bring me your shirts and pantaloons.'"

Mrs. Lincoln then went into the kitchen and returned with some cookies for the boys. Billie began to follow to the kitchen, but Mariah grabbed him by a shirt sleeve and stopped him. "You sit there and be quiet, if you can for a little while. Or I'll strap you!"

Mrs. Lincoln admonished Mariah. "Oh no you won't! I run this house and you're going to do as I say. Do you understand that, Mariah?"

Billie yelled loud as thunder: "Give it to her, Missy, with both barrels!"

"That pleasured de Missy," Mariah recalled, "and as black and dirty as Billie was, I thought sure she was gonna kiss him. From that very Gawd-blessed day on, her love my Billie-boy. And he was tooth and toenail for her. But I still thought I'd strap him, when we got home."

Mariah said that Mrs. Lincoln was really a fine housekeeper, keeping the house "clean as the driven snow." She also planted flowers, onions, lettuce, peas and more. Mariah said she shouldn't bend down to do any gardening, in her condition.

Mrs. Lincoln replied, "I would like to know who else would plant or dig up for us. Mister Lincoln is too tall to bend. He's bent so much already, carrying the boys straddled around his neck, bless them, playing piggyback."

Robert went up to his room and returned to the parlor with an armful of his clothes. Mrs. Lincoln told Billie to put some of them on, but Billie resisted.

"They're too fancy!" he complained.

Mariah took him to the shed, leading him by an ear as he screamed, "I don't want those sissy ruffly duds!"

Robert said to his mother, "You see, Ma? That's why they make fun of me and call me sissy!"

"Well, we'll see about some of the rest," said Mrs. Lincoln. She picked up the more plain shirts and gave them to Mariah with the dresses she had sewn for Julia.
She then said goodbye to Mariah and said she should only come every other washday, because she would do her own laundry in between visits.

Mrs. Lincoln then said, "Mariah, you and Billie have been who Bobby and I have needed all along. I feel I'm back home again in Lexington once again with Mammy Sally and her children."

Robert then asked, "Oh, Ma, can we call Mrs. Vance 'Mammy Mariah?'"

Mariah said, "That don't seem right. I's 'Mammy' to my younguns, but I was never 'Mammy' to no whites."

Mariah asked how old Mrs. Lincoln was and she said she was thirty-two. Mariah said she was just a year younger.

Mrs. Lincoln said to Mariah, "Maybe you wouldn't object if Bobby calls you 'Aunt Mariah.'"

Mariah brightened, liking that. "You's a powerful good lady, Mrs. Lincolumm."

Mrs. Lincoln smiled, knowing Mariah could never pronounce the name properly.

"You can continue calling me 'Missy," said Mrs. Lincoln, "as I've heard you call me to Billie. And Billie, you can call me 'Missy,' too. It sounds so sweet."

Mariah took Billie home in the cart and saw that Henry was worn out, from watching their four children.

Billie asked if he could have some flapjacks. He loved pancakes, and Mariah set about serving up piles of them for him, Henry, and their children.

While Billie shoveled down heaps of flapjacks with maple syrup, Mariah thought he looked happier than she had ever seen him.

"Billie's found a new friend," Mariah said to Henry.

Not stopping eating, Billie moved his head up and down with a big smile on his syrupy face.

Mariah said they quarreled about money matters often.

Robert left the house when they quarreled, and went to the barn. He and some new friends made a theater, with boxes to sit on, and made a stage curtain from material he found in the house.

Abe entered the barn and Robert pleaded with him, to take him and his friends to the woods so they could climb trees. He said he would, soon, then began hanging from a rafter by some rope and swung himself around. Robert and his friends watched he did a trick called "skin-the-cat," hanging upside-down.

After a while, he couldn't untangle himself, so Robert ran into the kitchen in the house and asked Mariah to get the meat cleaver and go to the barn with him. All his time, Mary was upstairs in her bedroom nursing another headache.

"When I git there, Mistah Abe war hangin' by the feet and haid, all tangle up."

She got him free and Abe, Robert, and the other boys all laughed. He then told the boys not to go into the house so they would not disturb his ailing wife, and promised to take them all to the woods when he returned from the circuit.

Mariah returned home later that day and told Henry about the skin-the-cat adventure. Billie looked mad, because his Ma had not taken him along that day and he missed out on all the fun with Mastah Robert.

Abraham Lincoln

"I am a bit of driftwood, all alone in the world," Abraham Lincoln once said regarding his feelings with his wife's family. This was reported by historian Stephen Berry in his 2007 book *House of Abraham: Lincoln and the Todd's, A Family Divided by War*.

Berry said Abe felt that way because his mother, brother, and sister had all died young, and his father saw him as a disappointment as a farmer. After his marriage to Mary Todd, from a wealthy and socially prominent family in Lexington, Kentucky, he was "awash" in internal family disputes.

His in-laws, the Todd's, were a family divided over the Civil War, about half supporting the Union and half supporting the Confederacy, and their differences affected Abe greatly. Many on both sides were killed in the war; brother against brother. But that was how most people described Lincoln, as being a lonely and melancholy man.

Abraham Lincoln was born in a one-room log cabin in Hodgenville, Kentucky on February 12, 1809. He was the second child of Thomas, a poor farmer, and Nancy Hanks Lincoln. Nancy Lincoln gave birth to a girl, Sarah, then a boy they named Abraham. Nancy Lincoln died of a milk sickness in 1818 when Abe was nine years old, and he grieved her death for the rest of his life.

A year later, Abe's father married a widow, Sarah "Sally" Bush Johnston, and she and Abe became very close. His sister Sarah died in 1828 while giving birth to a son who did not survive his birth. Abe now grieved over her death until his own.

Abe rarely went to school because his father needed him to help work their small farm. His father often criticized him for spending time "reading, scribbling, and writing poetry." Abe's favorite books were the *King James Bible, Aesop's Fables, The Pilgrim's Progress, Robinson Crusoe*, books on the life of President George Washington, and the autobiography of Benjamin Franklin, the statesman and inventor.

Abe helped work the family farm but also got odd jobs and gave those earnings to his father until he was twenty-one. His outside jobs were mainly cutting rails with an axe, for which he became called "The Rail-Splitter." Tall for his age, he was strong and enjoyed wrestling, especially in matches with a boy who was the leader of a group of what people called "ruffians," known as "the Clary's Grove boys."

Thomas Lincoln feared an epidemic of milk sickness in the area and moved the family to near Decatur, Illinois in 1830. Abe and his father had grown more distant from each other, mainly because Thomas discouraged him from becoming more educated. When Thomas decided to move the family again, Abe was old enough to go off on his own, so he did, settling in New Salem, Illinois. There he found work with some friends taking goods by flatboat to New Orleans, Louisiana by way of the Sangamon and Mississippi rivers. In New Orleans he witnessed slavery for the first time. He returned to New Salem, and remained living there for the next six years.

After moving to Illinois from Kentucky, he became a postmaster, surveyor, and a store owner. He served as a captain in the Black Hawk War of 1832. It was a brief conflict between the United States and American Indians led by Black Hawk, a Sauk Indian leader. It involved an Indian resettlement dispute which America won.

In New Salem, Abe shared rooms with a friend over an inn where he met and fell in love with the innkeeper's pretty daughter, Ann Rutledge. She reportedly encouraged him to become a lawyer, which he did become, although he was a self-educated and self-appointed lawyer.

Abe and Ann were in a relationship but did not become formally engaged, and she died at the age of 22 in 1835, reportedly of typhoid fever. Abe now grieved over her death, reportedly kneeling by her grave in cold rain for long hours. He reportedly suffered from "melancholy," a condition now referred to as clinical depression. The deaths of so many of his loved ones probably caused that.

Abe moved to Springfield, Illinois and in 1839, met Mary Todd, whose father was a wealthy slave-holding banker in Lexington, Kentucky, while she was visiting in Springfield.

By then Abe was a tall young man, six feet four inches, with long legs and a friendly look in his deep-set gray eyes. His black hair was usually tousled or uncombed, because of his habit of running his hand through it. Some considered his lean face to be ugly, but it usually reflected a friendly kindliness and inner warmth that softened his gaunt appearance.

By contrast, Mary Todd was short and stout, but had a pretty face. Her hair was a rich light-chestnut, her skin fair, and she had blue eyes. People described her as being "amiable" and "motherly,' and "an excitable and enthusiastic little woman."

Abe and Mary became engaged, but it was soon broken off, at his wish. About within a year, however, the couple reconciled and married on November 4, 1842 in her married sister's mansion in Springfield. Abe was not entirely happy about marrying Mary, and while getting dressed for the wedding, a friend asked where he was going. Abe replied, "To hell, I suppose."

After living in an apartment for two years after their marriage, when Robert was about nine months old Abe and Mary bought a house in Springfield. Lincoln called his first home a "little brown cottage." It was larger than that, a two-story frame house he bought for $1,500 in 1844 from the Rev. Charles Dresser, an Episcopal rector who had presided over the Lincolns' marriage in 1842.

Lincoln had become a lawyer by then and the house was near his law office. Their first child, Robert Todd Lincoln, was born in 1843, and their second son, Edward Baker Lincoln, called "Eddie," was born three years later. Abe was said be very fond of his children, and neither he nor Mary were very strict with them.

The Lincoln boys called their father "Pa" and their mother "Ma."

The Lincoln's fourth son, Thomas "Tad" Lincoln, was born on April 4, 1853, named after Abe's father. Mary had wished for a girl instead of a boy.

The early years of Willie and Tad were, according to historians, the happy or "garden" years of the Lincoln's lives. Tragically, the boys both died young, Willie of typhoid fever or heart failure at the age of 11 on February 20, 1862, just two years after his father's assassination. Tad died of pneumonia or tuberculosis nine years later in Chicago on July 15, 1871 when he was 18 years old.

Robert Lincoln was the only Lincoln child to live to adulthood. He had children, but his last descendant, great-grandson Robert Todd Lincoln Beckwith, died in 1985.

Lincoln had doubts about Robert when the boy was three years old. He thought him to be bright but perhaps would not live up to his potential and he showed signs of disapproving of him. If sensed by Robert, this assessment doubtless would have troubled and distanced him from his father. Sometimes, Robert ran away from home but was always found and returned home. He was at those times reprimanded and his mother would whip him,
no severely but to teach him not to run away again, but he would.

Robert Lincoln said very little about his boyhood in the Lincoln home in Springfield. He preferred to keep family matters private. So the most we know of his young years come from the recollections of Mariah Vance. She also told about the other Lincoln sons, Willie and Tad, whom she knew as the Lincolns' housekeeper in Springfield. She never went to Washington, D.C., so she knew nothing of their lives in the White House. Mary Lincoln's dressmaker in the White House, a black
woman named Elizabeth Keckley, wrote about what she heard and saw of the Lincolns there in a book she wrote after Abe's assassination.

Historians say Robert had a "distant relationship" with his father because during his boyhood years, Abe spent months away from home as a country lawyer on the judicial circuit. Their relationship was similar to that which Abe had with his father, but that was because his father disapproved of Abe spending so much of his time reading. Abe's father wanted him to work sun-up to sun-down on his small farm in Kentucky and then in Illinois.

Robert did say, in later years, "During my childhood and early youth, he [*his father*] was almost constantly away from home, attending court or making political speeches." He said that his most vivid image of his father was of Abe's packing his saddlebags to prepare for his travels through Illinois.

Abe, however, was proud of Robert and thought he was bright, but some historians say Abe saw him as something of a competitor.

Abe reportedly lacked the strong bond he had with his other sons, Willie and Tad, but Robert deeply admired his father and wept openly at his deathbed. More about Robert is in the following chapters.

Edward Baker "Eddie" Lincoln was born on March 10, 1846 in Springfield. A sickly child, he died before his fourth birthday on February 1, 1850.

William Wallace, nicknamed "Willie," was born on December 21, 1850. He became his father's favorite son. Willie and his younger brother Tad were considered to be "notorious hellions" when they lived in Springfield. Abe's law partner, William Herndon, wrote that the boys turned their law office in downtown Springfield "upside-down," pulling books off the shelves while their father appeared oblivious to their behavior.

Abe loved Willie and Tad, but Willie may have been his favorite. Both boys often climbed into his lap and patted his cheeks, then sometimes mischievously pulled his nose. When neighbors commented that they thought he was too lenient with them, he replied, "Let the children have a good time."

In 1854, Lincoln helped build a new Republican Party and four years later became its candidate for the U.S. Senate against Democrat Stephen A. Douglas. During their debates, Lincoln spoke out against the expansion of slavery in the United States. He lost the Senatorial election to Douglas, but ran against him for President in 1860 and won.

Lincoln had very little support in the election from those living in slaveholding states in the South and after his election, seven Southern slave states formed the Confederate States of America. War between the North and South began in the spring of 1861 and became known as a Civil War in the North and The War of Secession in the South as the Southern states chose to leave the Union. The long and bloody war began on April 12, 1861 and finally ended on May 9, 1865.

Lincoln and his wife were in a balcony box watching a play in Washington on the evening of April 14, 1865, a week before Easter on Good

Friday. Robert declined an invitation to join them, saying he was tired after spending much of his time in a covered wagon at a battlefront in the war. He had asked his father repeated to let him serve in the army, but Abe said he needed him for other duties.

Near the end of the play in Ford's Theater, a disgruntled and perhaps deranged actor, John Wilkes Booth, came up behind Abe with a pistol and shot him in the back of the head. Lincoln was taken from the theater to a bed in a house across the street where he died the next morning, his assassination shocking the world. He had been 56 years old.

Booth was later caught after trying to flee, and when he refused to give himself up, a soldier shot and killed him. He had been a Confederate sympathizer opposed to the abolition of slavery. He hated Lincoln for restoring the Union and after the President signed the Emancipation Proclamation ending slavery in America.

Between Lincoln's assassination and her sons' deaths, Mary Lincoln suffered so emotionally that Robert feared for her safety, so he had her temporarily committed to a mental health asylum in 1875. She was later released and returned to Springfield where she died on July 6, 1882.

Abraham, Mary, Eddie, Willie, and Tad Lincoln are all buried in a tomb in Oak Ridge Cemetery in Springfield. Robert is interred in Arlington National Cemetery in Arlington, Virginia, together with his wife and their son Jack, who died at the age of 16 from food poisoning.

Robert Lincoln became president of the Pullman Palace Car Company that made train cars. He served as the 35th U.S. Secretary of War from 1881 to 1885 in the administrations of Presidents James Garfield and Chester A. Arthur and was the U.S. ambassador to the United Kingdom from 1889 to 1893 during the presidency of Benjamin Harrison. He also was a dedicated amateur astronomer and an avid golfer. He died on July 26, 1926 at the age of 82.

Ironically, Robert Lincoln was present at the assassination of President James A. Garfield on July 2, 1881. Charles J. Guiteau shot him to death on a street in Washington, D.C. Garfield had invited Robert to attend a ceremony there.

Robert also was present when President William McKinley was fatally shot on September 6, 1901. McKinley had invited Robert to join him and some others at the Pan-American Exposition in Buffalo, New York, where Garfield was assassinated by Leon Czolgosz.

Robert reportedly received another presidential invitation later and declined. He commented: "No, I'm not going, and they better not ask me, because there is a certain fatality about presidential functions when I am present."

Most ironically, however, Robert Lincoln had been saved from possible serious injury or death by Edwin Booth, brother of Lincoln's assassin, John Wilkes Booth.

In late 1863 or early 1864, Robert was on a train platform in Jersey City, New Jersey. He had been among people who had been on the platform to purchase late-night train tickets from the conductor. The eager people crowded together before the conductor, when the train began moving. Lincoln lost his footing and began falling into the moving train.

He later said, "I was twisted off my feet and had dropped somewhat, with feet downward. I was personally helpless, when my coat collar was vigorously seized and I was quickly pulled up and out to a secure footing on the platform. Upon turning to thank my rescuer, I saw it was Edwin Booth [*a stage actor*], whose face was of course well-known to me. I expressed my gratitude to him, and in doing so, called him by name."

Edwin Booth had not known that he had saved the life of President Lincoln's son. Both later felt that the incident was of some comfort to Edwin after his brother had shot and killed Lincoln.

A Hair-Raising Adventure

Mariah returned to the Lincoln's home the following Monday washday. While she was working in the shed, Mrs. Lincoln approached.

"Bobby's eyes are slightly crossed," she said. "He's had an operation, but I'm not sure his eyes are well enough for him to return to school in the fall."

"He'd miss not schoolin', Missy," Mariah replied.

Mrs. Lincoln said she hadn't had time to decide. "I've been so busy this past week. I've sewn curtains for the entire house, made clothes for Bobby, if he does return to school in the fall, and clothes for the new baby that is coming. I hope it is a girl. Mister Lincoln and I would both love to have a girl."

"I's wanting mine to be a boy!" said Mariah.

"Why, Mariah!" said Mrs. Lincoln, "why didn't you tell me you too are expecting a child?"

Mariah replied that her condition did not show up until she had weaned Julia.

"Why didn't you bring Billie with you today?" asked Mrs. Lincoln. "I've fixed over the clothes he called 'sissy.' You must bring him the next time. Maybe Bobby will stay home a while, if Billie is here to play with. I never know where he is, or what he's doing when his father is away at work, and that is most of the time."

Mariah finished the laundry and left, but returned in two weeks. It was now June and she brought Billie with her. Abe had come back home from the circuit riding.

Billie was out front of the house with his mother and Abe, throwing a ball against the house and catching it on its return.

"Where's Bobby?" Billie asked.

Abe pointed to the upstairs. He then caught the ball and he and Billie played the game for a while. When Abe had tired, they sat on the woodpile near the barn. Billie squirmed as he sat, and scratched his head. Abe noticed and asked Mariah,

"What's Bill digging up there for?" He always called him Bill, not Billie.

Said Mariah, "I swear he catched some lice from playing with the bad white trash scamps next door to us."

Abe put a hand in Billie's thick head of black hair and caught a louse and cracked it with his fingers.

"Mariah, I know the very fellow who can get rid of these lice in a hurry," said Abe, "if you'll let me take Bill to him to my barber."

Mariah agreed and Abe took Billie to his barber in town. Robert wanted to go along, but Mrs. Lincoln was afraid he'd catch Billie's lice.

Abe returned home with Billie within an hour and Mariah nearly fainted, looking at her son. He was totally bald. The barber, a black man, had solved Billie's hair problem by shaving it all off.

Robert saw his friend's bald head and Mariah told him what had happened. He didn't laugh, but a big smile crossed his face. She had a sock cap with her and pushed it over Billie's head.

Robert then took Billie by an arm and ran out of the house with him. They headed for the barn, when Billie stumbled, not seeing very well with the woolen cap falling over his eyes. He nearly fell, but Robert held him up and they played sock ball throw-and-catch in the back yard.

On the cart ride home, Mariah wondered how she was going to explain Billie's bald head. When Henry saw him without the cap, he wailed, "What happened to his fine head of wooly hair?"

He put Billie over his knees and spanked him. Mariah explained that their son's hair was alive with lice from the boys next door and that Mr. Lincoln took him to his barber who shaved all his hair off. Henry then let up on Billie and their boy ran out of the house.

Henry did not forgive Abe for days, then finally did in the weeks that followed as Billie's hair began to grow back.

Billie decided that the lice had done some good for him. It taught him not to hang around the white boys next door any more.

Mary Todd Lincoln

While Abe was born in a one-room log cabin in Kentucky, his future wife Mary Todd was born in a 14-room mansion in the same state. They were opposites in many ways.

She was born Mary Ann Todd on December 13, 1818, the fourth of seven children in a large, wealthy family in Lexington, Kentucky. Her parents were Robert Smith Todd, a banker, and Elizabeth Parker Todd. The Todd's were slaveholders, and Mary was reared in comfort and refinement, totally the opposite of Abe.

Her mother died when she was six, and two years later her father married Elizabeth "Betsy" Humphreys and they had nine children together. Mary and her stepmother had a difficult relationship, as Abe did with his father. In that they were alike. He also was tall and lanky while Mary was short and stout, but had a pretty face. Abe was not good-looking; his face was gaunt.

Mary, also unlike Abe, was well-educated. She attended a finishing school for young ladies of society during her teen years, learning to speak French fluently and studied dance, drama, music, and social graces. By the age of 20 she was considered to be witty and out-going, easy with people, and had a good grasp of politics. Like her parents, she was a member of the Whig Party which later became the Republican Party to which Abe belonged.

After graduating from finishing school, Mary then moved to Springfield, Illinois in October, 1839 to live with her married sister, Elizabeth Edwards, whose doctor husband Ninian was the son of a former governor.

The move was probably both to get away from her stepmother and to find a husband in Springfield. She was courted by Abe's long-time political opponent, Democrat Stephen A. Douglas, until her marriage to Abe. Reportedly, she had a near obsession to become First Lady of the United States and saw more potential in Abe becoming president, if she worked hard enough to push him in that direction.

Abe and Mary Todd were married on November 4, 1842 at her sister's home when she was 23 while Abe was ten years older.

During Lincoln's years as a lawyer in towns on the Illinois circuit, Mary was often left at home for months to raise the children and run the house. This load without Lincoln's help caused her often to suffer from migraine headaches and some severe illnesses, as well as depression at times. The headaches were not helped by a later fall from a carriage from which she suffered a head injury while living in the White House.

The Todd's were from a border state where slavery was permitted. Several of her half-brothers served in the Confederate Army and were killed in action, while one brother served the Confederacy as an Army surgeon. Mary staunchly supported Abe in his efforts as President to save the Union and was strictly loyal to his policies. She worked hard at being First Lady but some criticized her manners as "coarse and pretentious."

Mary Lincoln refurbished the White House which included extensive redecorating of all the public and private rooms and bought new china for their tables. Abe, who always criticized her for spending money unwisely, was angered at the bills she ran up for these things in the White House, even though Congress was paying for them.

During her years in the White House, Mary Lincoln often visited hospitals around Washington to give flowers and fruit to wounded Civil War soldiers. She also wrote letters for them to send to their loved ones. Sometimes she went with Lincoln to visit camps in the field.

As the Civil War ended and the Union was united again, in April 1865, she expected to continue as the First Lady when the nation was at peace. On the morning of Friday, April 14, Abe woke up more cheerful than he had been for some time. He walked around the White House and told staff that he was feeling happy. Mary thought that saying such things out loud was back luck.

Mary wanted to see a play that evening, a comedy at Ford's Theater. As they sat watching the play, Lincoln whispered that he wanted to visit the Holy Land, saying there is no place that he so much desired to see as Jerusalem. They were his last words to her. A few minutes later, John Wilkes Booth, a stage actor, entered their balcony box, came up behind him, and shot President Lincoln in the back of the head.

Mary had been holding Abe's hand affectionately when the bullet struck. She accompanied others as her mortally wounded husband was taken across the street to the home of a family named Petersen where he was taken to a bedroom.

Lincoln's Cabinet members were summoned and they gathered around his bed. Robert Lincoln sat with his father throughout the night until the President died the following morning, Saturday, April 15, 1865. Secretary Edwin M. Stanton ordered Mary from the room because she was so distraught with grief and most likely was in shock.

After Abe's assassination, Mary received messages of condolence from all over the world, many of which she tried to answer personally. To England's Queen Victoria she wrote, "I have received the letter which Your Majesty has had the kindness to write. I am deeply grateful for this expression of tender sympathy, coming as they do, from a heart which from its own sorrow, can appreciate the intense grief I now endure." The queen had suffered the death of her beloved husband, Prince Albert, just four years earlier.

Now a widow, Mary returned to Illinois and lived in Chicago with her sons.

In 1868 Mary's former dressmaker and confidante, Elizabeth Keckley (1818-1907) published a book, *Behind the Scenes, or, Thirty Years a Slave, and Four Years in the White House.*

Mrs. Keckley found no American publishing house would publish her book, so she had it published in England. Keckley had been born a slave but bought her freedom and that of her son and became a successful business woman in Washington.

Mary considered Keckley's book to be a breach of their friendship. The book, which originally met with criticism largely for that reason, has since been accepted by many historians and biographers and has been quoted to describe Abe's and Mary's lives while in the White House. Ms. Keckley never knew Mariah Vance or of her memoirs of the Lincolns in Springfield.

Mary wore only black after Abe's death, She walked around Chicago with $56,000 in government bonds sewn into her petticoats. Despite the money she had, she had an irrational fear of being poor.

The death of her son Tad on July 15, 1871, following the death of her husband and two of her other sons, left Mary with overpowering grief and depression. Robert, then a rising young lawyer in Chicago, became alarmed at her increasingly erratic behavior. In March 1875, during a visit to Jacksonville, Florida, Mary became convinced that Robert was deathly ill. Hurrying back to Chicano, she found him to be healthy.

One day, she thought the house was on fire and nearly jumped out of a window to escape. Robert then decided that for her own safety, she needed to be institutionalized.

On May 20, 1975 Robert reluctantly committed her to a private asylum in Batavia, Illinois. She wrote to her lawyer and to the editor of the *Chicago Times* to help her get released. Three months after being committed, she was declared well enough to go to Springfield to live with her sister Elizabeth, as she had desired. She became estranged from Robert when he had her institutionalized, and many criticized him for his action. Mother and son did not reconcile until shortly before her death.

Mary then spent the next four years traveling throughout Europe and then lived in Pau, France. Her health and eyesight failed and she began falling a lot. In 1879 she fell from a stepladder and suffered spinal cord injuries. She lived on a few more years, but lapsed into a coma at her sister's home in Springfield and died on July 6, 1882 at the age of 63. She was buried in the Lincoln tomb in Oak Ridge Cemetery in Springfield alongside her husband and with her children, except Robert, the only son to survive Abe and Mary.

The Fishing Party

Mariah was back at the Lincoln's, doing their wash in the tub in the back yard on the Second of July. She looked up to see Billie spitting out a cood of tobacco. She boxed his ears and he yelped. That brought Abe out of the house.

"Mistah Abe, I caught Billie chewin' tobacco," she said.

Abe looked at Billy. "I wondered what's got you this time. Maybe a horse fly?"

Abe then tried to cover for Billie. "Mariah, Bill surely had his mouth full of licorice candy, so he spit part of it out."

"No, Mistah Abe," she countered. "See the cood at you big toe?"

She hadn't noticed until then that Abe was barefoot. She thought they were "the most awful feet I ever seen. Besides being two times as big as they oughta be, they had bumps all over."

Abe Lincoln went barefooted as much as he could, reminding him of his boyhood in Kentucky. His feet perspired and he wore shoes or boots as seldom as he could. When he did wear them, he put newspapers in them, to absorb the sweat.

Abe explained, "When barefooted, I feel more at home."

Billie then spit out the tobacco he had been chewing. Mariah said it was his first experience in that bad habit.

Abe then took a ten dollar bill out of his pants pocket and gave it to Mariah. She was amazed, thinking she had never had that much money in her hand at one time.

"I'm leaving for Chicago tomorrow or the next," he said. "I have business there and will attend the United States District Court meeting. I believe Mrs. Lincoln will be looking for you and Bill while I'm away."

Robert thought about that. He and Billie wanted their fathers to take them fishing over at the Sangamon river near town, but they were always too busy. Perhaps the real reason was, Abe did not fish. He thought of fish being like animals and he never hunted animals.

Nonetheless, an idea began to hatch in the boys' heads. They talked about it in the Lincoln barn where Robert taught Billie how to read and work with numbers. Mariah and Henry had become proud of Billie's learning. It was against the law for whites to teach blacks to read or write, but Robert did it anyway, on the sly.

Mariah put dinner on the table for Henry and their children, and Billie asked his father, "Pappy, when we goin' fishin'? Tomorrow?"

Henry said," If you think I's about to walk six mile to hold a string in da watah, you's plain dumb!"

Mariah chided Henry and called *him* dumb. "You sure can do that much for your boy what wants to be educated."

Henry relented and Mariah made them a packet of corn meal bread and sow meat to take along on their fishing trip early the next morning in the Sangamon River, on the Third of July. Henry made fishing poles and pin hooks for him and Billie. In the morning, they dug up some squirming worms.

They went fishing that day and came back home as the sun was about to set, each holding a string of about eight fat fish. Tired as they were, father and son then cleaned them to prepare them for supper.

While they cleaned the fish, Billie said, "I bet Mistah Abe and Mastah Bobby wish they had some of the fish Mastah Robert catch and they give to us."

Henry and Billie had fished in separate parts along the river. Now Henry realized that Billie had not been alone.

"Billie, what you been up to?" asked Henry. "How come Mistah Abe and Mastah Robert was fishin' there with you? No wonder you knowed just when to start this mornin.'"

Henry decided he knew what had gone on down by the river and that Billie and Robert had planned to meet there all along.

He remembered and told Mariah, "First, when we get to the ribber, Billie wants to climb a tree. I say, 'Go 'head.' He climb the tree to da top and look 'round. Den come down slow, all tuckered. Then he put both two fingers in his mouth and whistle sich a Gawd-awful loud blow, 'bout scared me stiff!

"Just then, not so far off was a whistle. I knew it warn't a bird answerin.' Somethin' war up.'"

Billie said, "Mastah Bobby got his Pappy to go fishin' down on the Sangamon same time us this mornin.' Dey caught the first fish and keep getting' more. They sure have a good long fish pole, and cooked bait with meat, cotton, corn meal, and sweet oil."

Henry asked Billie, "Did Mistah Abe know you scamps was plannin' to go fishin' together this morning?"

Billie did not reply, but a wide smile crossed his face.

Henry wanted to know if both he and Mr. Lincoln had been victims of a plot by their sons. Abe wondered the same thing and on the morning of the Fourth of July when

Mariah brought Billie to the Lincoln house, he asked Robert to tell the truth about the fishing trip.

"I've a crow to pick with you two boys,:" said Abe, "and I want to pick it here before your two mothers. When you two rascals put for the barn, it isn't all for reading, writing, and arithmetic. Understand this first... I want you two to be good friends. I'm more than glad you want to learn, Bill. And Bobby, you're willing to teach him what you've already learned and it's fresh in your mind."

The boys wondered what was going to come next.

Abe said on: "I want you two to have all the fun life holds for you, unless that includes trickery and scheming, as you pulled over on Mister Vance and me about a fishing party for four."

Robert explained. "Pa, Billie and I didn't trick or scheme. He wanted so much to go to the woods with us the other day. But you didn't insist, and Aunt Mariah wouldn't let him. She told him he should know his place with white folks."

Abe wondered what Robert was leading up to.

Robert continued: "I told Billie I was going to try to get you to take me fishing. That was while I was teaching him numbers and letters in the barn. He was writing them down and I was waiting until he got through copying the twenty-six letters and ten figures I had set down for him to learn from.

"Well, Billie jumped up and he almost cried, that he wanted his Pappy to take him fishing, too. I told him that if his Pappy knew how hard he was trying to learn, maybe he would take him fishing. 'Well,' he said, 'If I can get him to go, maybe we can meet you and your Pa at the river."

It was starting to make sense to Abe, as Mrs. Lincoln and Mariah listened.

Robert continued: "So I said, 'If we could both start about the same time, maybe eight o'clock tomorrow morning, we might get there at the same time.' But I knew, Pa, your legs were longer than Mister Vance's, even if you do walk dragging them. And I knew Billie's Pappy was mad at you for having Billie's hair all cut off."

Abe was growing impatient for the suspect on trial in court to explain his defense.

"So those were two problems that presented themselves," said Robert. "I don't know what Billie did when he got home, but the last problem must have been worked out satisfactorily, for when we met at the river, Mister Vance seemed to like you, Pa."

"And I like him," said Abe. "Now get on with your defense."

"Billie said to me," Robert went on, "'Maybe we would reach the river at different places.' I said he could whistle. If he didn't see me, I would answer his whistle. That was all there was to it. Now where do you find a scheme or a trick?"

"Well," said Abe, "I want you two boys to be good friends always. But I was beginning to think you were bad for each other. I see now how wrong I was, and apologize."

"What's 'pologize' mean?" Billie asked.

Said Abe, "That's one way of saying I'm sorry. But it wouldn't have been too hard for you, Bobby, or you, Bill, to have put confidence in your Pappy and me."

"What's 'con'dence?'" Billie asked.

"That word was a little too big. It means both you and Bobby could have told your Pappy and me your plans to meet at the river"

Said Billie, "Dat warn't Mastah Robert's fault. I knew my Pappy war mad at you, Mastah Lincoln, on 'count of my haircut, 'cause he called you a scarecrow."

Abe laughed. "That's what I am, Bill. But you did scheme a little, didn't you?

"I thought my Pappy wouldn't go, or if he did, he'd sock you."

"Thanks, Bill. You're a real protector. But always remember to try kindness before you try your fists."

Abe told Mrs. Lincoln and Robert that he would take them to the fairgrounds for the 4th of July parade and fireworks. Billie tugged at his mother's arm and she knew what he was thinking about to ask. "We'll go too," Mariah said. "But your father and the other chilluns will go by ourselves and be at another part of the fairgrounds."

Billie thought that when they got there, he might whistle for Master Robert.

Eddie Lincoln

The second son born to Abraham and Mary Todd Lincoln was Edward Baker Lincoln, born in Springfield on March 10, 1846 and named after Abe's friend and political associate Edward Dickinson Baker. Abe and Mary both spelled his name "Eddy," but the National Park Service used "Eddie," which is on his gravestone in Springfield. He died in Springfield on February 1, 1850.

Abe wrote to a friend, Joshua Speed: "We have another boy. He is very much such a child as Bob was at his age, rather of a longer order."

Little is known about Eddie, and Mariah Vance never knew him because he died a few months before she began working in the Lincoln home. Eddie's parents described him as a tender-hearted, kind, and loving child.

One story regarding Eddie is that one day while with his mother and brother Robert, visiting her family in Lexington, Kentucky in the spring of 1848, Robert found a stray kitten and brought it to him. Mary did not like cats and ordered that it be thrown out. Eddie, who most always got what he wanted if he was insistent upon it, screamed and protested so he was able to keep the kitten which he cared for and loved.

Eddie Lincoln was never a healthy child. He was ill during much of the time his father was serving in Congress as a member of the U.S. House of Representatives in Washington, D.C. He periodically showed signs of improvement, but was suffering from a chronic illness that turned out to be tuberculosis.

Eddie's final days began the day before his mother's 31st birthday. He developed a dangerously high fever and had bad coughing fits that left him exhausted. Unable to eat or rest, nothing seemed to ease his suffering. Springfield doctors thought that was from diphtheria, but he most likely was in the final stages of pulmonary, or lung, tuberculosis, commonly called consumption.

Consumption killed more Americans in 1850 than any other disease. Half of its victims were under the age of five. The disease was contracted from drinking polluted water or tainted food.

Eddie lingered on for 52 days, then died before his fourth birthday, on a cold and rainy morning, February 1, 1850. His mother reportedly cried throughout his final night. The next day, Rev. Smith conducted Eddie's funeral in the Lincoln home.

Something to Crow About

"That winter war long," Mariah recalled, "but pass [*into the Spring of 1851*]. It seem Henry have lot of hauling for stove wood. He haul the Lincolumns about eight or ten cords. The poles, Mastah Abe chopped himself. People never forgot Mistah Abe war a woodchopper. I always wonder what so strange-like about that."

Mariah said Robert came home from school often saying boys bullied him about his father being a rail-splitter and now a woodchopper for their stove.

"But Mastah Robert have such a tender heart, and would never say things tit-for-tat to them who tormented him. And he warn' stuck up [*as some people said*]. "He come to my house whenever in Danville [*when she and Henry and their children moved there after the Lincolns went to Washington*]. "And he ate corn pone at my table [*years later, as an adult*]."

Mariah then recalled how Abe reacted to Robert saying that some people criticized his father for being a woodchopper. He took Robert by the hand and gave him some advice on bullying.

"Son I'm not ashamed of any honest labor I ever did, or am I ashamed I am a son of a common, illiterate, laboring father. They have all been stepping-stones to the better life I now enjoy. So son, just push all that teasing those youngsters are up to, in the back of your mind. Just feel sorry for them. They are foolish and the losers, not you."

Easter came and Robert was home from school for a spring vacation. He attended a school in Springfield run by Abel W. Estabrook. Abe was about to go on the circuit again, but before leaving, he went to a room off the parlor which had been set up as the baby's nursery. Abe took Willie out the crib, which was old-fashioned and looked like it had been carved out of a hollow log. It was cut with a hood at the head and a set of rockers on the bottom.

"De Missy have it all flub-dub-up," said Mariah. "That Willie war dress like I dress my girl babies. Maybe de Missy want a girl so bad, was why her dress him that way.

"Mastah Abe walk 'round about the house carryin' Willie on his shoulders. He kiss Willie, and for the first time since I knowed them, he kiss de Missy.

"Mastah Robert walk to the barn with his Pa until he hitch his horse 'Buck,' then come runnin' back in the house for his Pa's stovepipe hat. He carry it up to his Pa with the top down, so as not to spill out Mastah Abe's papers inside. Dat's the only time I did know of Mistah Abe leavin' his hat. Must have had a heal of somethin' on his mind to forget that hat."

Mariah said she went to the Lincoln's home every two weeks that spring and that Mary had thrown a lot of parties.

"Mastah Robert and my Billie was in the shed, 'cause it war too cold to play in the barn. They manage to keep quiet until I went to the kitchen to clean there while the clothes dry outside. They froze dry.

"De Missy have knitted a pair of mittens for each of my chillun and me, too. That took a lot of knittin.' And they bought a pair of those horsehide gloves lined with wool for Henry. Those new wool yarn mittens sure keep my hands warm when I takin' down the clothes."

Mariah then recalled that Billie did not get much learning from Robert, and that Jim Crow got the learning. Those boys say 'Stop!' so often, that crow learn to say 'Stop! Stop! Stop!' Mastah Robert laugh 'til he cry. He beg his Ma to let him have his pals to come and hear, but she say, 'Another day.'" her foot down. She say, 'If Billie stays, the rest of the gang will get here some way, and the house will be overrun with boys. Wait until some warm day when you can all go to the barn."

Mariah said, "I stirred up a batch of crackin' bread with fresh chops and gravy sop for their dinner. I want to put off for home then, to get my Henry and chilluns something hot to eat. Mastah Robert coax me to let Billie stay, but de Missy put

De Missy then tell Mastah Robert he have to practice his recitin' for the Christmas Eve at the Presbyterian church they attended. "He done grumbled, but started upstairs."

Mariah said Mrs. Lincoln took the boys to church every Sunday, but Abe seldom joined them. As a lawyer, he represented some of the men and women who were in church but who had not paid his store-owning clients for the things they bought, especially the dresses, hats, and shoes the fine-dressed ladies wore at the church services. He considered them to be hypocrites.

Mariah then continued with her story about the black crow. Jim Crow then flew onto Abe and he patted it and brushed down its feathers as it caw-cawed. Billie then held out his arm and the crow flew to him. The crow then swooped at Robert and he covered his head with his hands, but it just landed on top his head. "Mastah Robert laugh so loud and long," said Mariah, "this no lie, that black crow laugh, too!"

Abe said, "I hate to cage that bird. But our six cats, especially the black tom, will have to be tamed a little more, as well as the crow. Jim Crow may come up missing its wings and tail, and the tom may have his eyes pecked out. If anything should happen to the little kittens, I know Mister Crow would have to go back to the woods."

He said on: "Mrs. Lincoln doesn't care too much for the noise of the crow, as Willie, the precious little rascal, is here and mustn't be disturbed. Since a cat jumped into the crib with Willie, she keeps them out in the shed or barn. I suspect the shed is where Mister Crow will have to go."

Abe said that his pet turtle was hibernating somewhere for the winter. He had it tied up in the barn, but it got away by breaking the rope that held it.

Mariah took Billie home and made corn cakes and cooked some chickens Abe had given her.

"We have a meal as fine as anyone's Christmas dinner. That chicken with chicken sop and some flud-dub food from Willie's birthday party was licked up clean by we'ns."

Weeks and months passed and Mariah recalled the autumn of 1852. Abe had returned from another two months on the circuit, and Mary told Mariah she was afraid that when Robert played with Willie, he might hurt him. entertaining children. I believe Mastah Lincoln had so few play days with other children when he was a child, he is fulfilling that longing now. At times, he acts like a child."

"He don't mean to be rough," said Mary. "He has played with some very rough boys and has learned from them. Then, too, he tries to emulate his father, or perhaps surpass his father's stunts of entertaining children. I believe Mister Lincoln had so few play days with other children when he was a child, he is fulfilling that longing now. At times, he acts like a child."

Mary said on: "Robert tries to imitate his father in games such as piggy-backs. Then he jumps with Willie on his shoulders, something I've never seen Mister Lincoln do. He takes him by one hand and whirls him around in a circle. The last time, I caught him trying to teach Willie how to slide down the stars banister. It's all in play, but I just had to reprimand Robert. I wanted him to understand the danger to baby Willie's life and limbs, and told him he isn't as grown up as he thinks he is."

Mariah listened without commenting as Mrs. Lincoln said more.

"Mister Lincoln says if I keep on picking at Robert, he'll eventually resent it keenly. Either by withdrawing from me, then seeking the company who may mislead him. Or perhaps withdrawing into his shell, thereby becoming a stranger."

Mary said she knows that Robert loves Willie and wants him to be a companion. "He needs Willie, and Willie needs him."

Mary Lincoln gave birth to her fourth son, Thomas Lincoln, on April 4, 1853, and he was named after Abe's father. Her brother-in-law Doctor Wallace examined him and reported: "He has a large head."

Abe joked and called the baby "Tadole," because his head was so much larger compared to the normal size of his body or legs. The Lincolns named their newborn son "Tad."

Mariah said, "De Missy get excited and say, 'Oh my, oh my! Is my baby deformed?'"

"He's a fine baby," replied Dr. Wallace. "A really beautiful child."

However, Tad was born with a cleft palate and when he talked later, it was with a lisp and he could hardly be understood. He could only swallow liquid food, so his mother chewed whole foods such as chicken and meat and potatoes and then fed it to him.

Mariah said that Tad took such a long time to walk and talk, everyone feared that he never would do either. But he eventually did both and soon he and Willie were playmates. When the weather warned, they played together in the back yard. They became pals, but when Robert came home from school and wanted to play with him, Tad often bit him when he came near.

"Once, Taddie have a big welt on him, and de Missy claim Mastah Robert have hit him or pinched him. I searched and found a great big bed bug in Taddie's crib. As clean as de Missy war, I declare I don't know where it come from. When her asked me, I war right smart mad and was goin;' home and never come back.

"Then she accuse Mistah Abe of bringin' the bed bug home from one of the 'dirty taverns' he lodged in on the circuit."

Mistah Abe say, "Well, Mother, if little Taddie never gets anything worse than a bed bug bite, he'll come out in tip-top shape. I've had worse bites from vicious tongues."

Ruth Painter Randall tells the following in her book, *Lincoln's Sons*, reporting from many sources:

Taking walks with babies was mainly women's work in those days, but Abe enjoyed taking Willie and baby Tad in a little red wagon for outings up and down the street on which their house stood. He usually pushed their wagon with one hand while holding a book in his other, and reading it. He became so engrossed in his reading that on one occasion, when baby Tad fell out of the wagon, he hadn't noticed until Mrs. Lincoln heard the infant crying and came out of the house to rush to him. It became a family joke for some time.

Willie was three or four years old when Mrs. Lincoln left him unattended for a few minutes after giving him a bath. He loved the freedom of being without clothes, so he ran out of he house naked. He ran up the street and ducked under a fence and into a green field.

Abe was sitting on the front porch when Willie dashed out of the house in his birthday suit and was amused. He did not go after him until Mrs. Lincoln noticed her boy had gone out, and ordered Abe to find him. Abe crossed the field and found him, then hoisted Willie onto his shoulders, kissed him, and took him home where the boy got another bath.

Neighbors sometimes criticized Abe for carrying Todd on his shoulder on walks to his law office. A woman once said, "Why, Mr. Lincoln, put down that great big boy. He's big enough to walk." Abe replied amiably, "Oh, don't you think his little feet get too tired?"

One day, Abe gave Tad a knife and asked him to show it to a friend. Tad hesitated and Abe asked, "You haven't lost the knife, have you?" Tad replied sheepishly, "Bob told me if he was me, he'd swap my knife for candy."

Lincoln laughed, then asked Robert, "Bob, how much did you pay for that candy?" Bob named the price, and his father said, "Why, Tad's knife costs three bits. Do you think you made a fair trade with Tad?" Bob looked ashamed and said, "No sir," then took the knife out of his pocket and gave it to Tad.

Lincoln then told Tad to return the candy to Robert, but Tad said he had eaten it all and had no money to give his brother. Abe solved the problem by giving Tad a coin and Tad said to Robert, "Come on, Bob, I'll get your candy back for you," then led him to a store.

Sometimes Abe took Willie and Tad and some of the neighborhood boys in his carriage and drove them out to the Sangamon River for a picnic. He told them exciting tales about hunters, settlers, and Indians, and played games with them, including marbles and blind man's bluff, or showed him how good he was at spinning a top.

Robert Lincoln

Abe and Mary Lincoln's first-born of four sons, Robert Todd Lincoln, was born on August 1, 1843 at their home in Springfield. He was named after his mother's father, Robert S. Todd, an influential banker of Lexington, Kentucky.

Robert grew up to be five feet nine and a half inches tall, some six and a half inches shorter than his father. His left eye turned slightly inward, so he looked a little cross-eyed. Like his father, Robert had a slight dimple in his chin, and his skin also was dark. His face was rounder than Abe's, more like his mother's. Robert also was shy, unlike his younger brothers Willie and Tad.

While Robert also was spoiled and indulged in by his parents as a boy, he did not have the same closeness his brothers had with his father. There always seemed to be an emotional wall between Robert and his father.

Robert became Mariah Vance's favorite while she was the Lincoln's laundress and housekeeper for ten years in their home in Springfield. He met her son Billie when both boys were almost eight years old the second time Mariah came to work the Lincoln house. Robert and Billie became instant best friends, remaining close until Abe became President and the family moved to Washington. Abe and Mary encouraged the boys' friendship and both of them also liked Billie very much.

Robert Lincoln said very little about his boyhood in the Lincoln home in Springfield. He preferred to keep family matters private. The most we know of his young years come from the recollections of Mariah Vance. She also told about the other Lincoln sons, Willie and Tad, whom she often saw in and around the house, often getting playfully into mischief.

Robert, however, shy as he was, did not always shy away from mischief. When he was a boy, he and some friends tried to train some dogs in the neighborhood to do some tricks for a show they were to put on. They wanted the dogs to stand on their hind feet and growl, but got no response. So they tied a rope around the dogs' necks and over a rafter in the Lincoln barn. Hearing howling and screams from the barn, a neighbor alerted Abe who rushed to the barn and freed the dogs as Robert and his friends ran off. It was one of the rare times that Abe reprimanded any of his sons.

Robert Lincoln visited the Vance's often the summer and fall of 1851, and again during the year that followed. Mariah thought it was partly so he could visit her and Billie, but also because his mother kept sending him out of the house so he and his friends did not make any noise to disturb her of baby Willie.

Mariah asked about the baby and Robert said it had had the colic, but recovered.

"But he still holds his breath, sometimes until he's blue in the face. That scares Ma."

Robert was by then teaching all of Mariah's children to read and write.

During the seasons that passed, Abe often brought home stray animals, among them some cats and a crow that he gave to Billie to keep as a pet. Mariah said Abe named the black bird "Jim Crow." It was not named after a person, but a popular minstrel song that stereotyped blacks. It came to personify the government-sanctioned racial oppression and segregation in the United States at that time.

Mariah allowed Billie to keep the bird, but complained that it was either always under her feet in the shack or eating off the table. She also disliked the crow because it made a lot of noise, too, "caw, cawing."

Mary looked like she was going to have another headache, so Abe took one of the boys under one arm and the other under his other arm and took them outside. Peace and quiet had returned to the Lincoln home, if only temporarily.

Mariah was expecting again. She soon delivered her eleventh child, a girl she and Henry named Lydia Narcissa.

A friend of the Lincoln's in Springfield, Joseph R. Kent, said, "Bob, the elder, and Tad the younger, were Mama boys. They neither one had the slightest personal appearance or deliberate easy manner of Mr. Lincoln. They both resembled their mother in looks and actions. Will was the true picture of Mr. Lincoln, in every way, even to carrying his head slightly inclined toward his left shoulder."

While in later years, Robert Lincoln tried to preserve his father's legacy, he was perhaps least like his father. Robert was more shy, reserved, and more concerned with public appearances.

He did not like public attention; at best he merely endured it. He nevertheless developed a very keen sense of propriety. He spent much more time with his mother's side of the family than did his brothers and his temperament was said to be more Todd than Lincoln. An age difference of seven and 10 years separated him from his younger siblings so he was chronologically distanced from them as well.

It has been speculated that Robert was jealous of the attention his parents gave to Willie and Tad. Before they were born, he had had their parental attention. Now he had to share that with his two younger brothers and may have felt virtually ignored.

When Robert was just a year old, he was bitten by a dog who was said to be mad and there was a danger that he could contract rabies or hydrophobia. In those times, a so-called "mad stone" was applied to the wound, to draw out the poison. Abe took him to Terre Haute, Indiana, the nearest place such treatment could be found. Soaking the wound in milk seemed to work and Robert recovered.

Robert's boyhood were sometimes lean financial years for the Lincoln's and he had to have the seat of his pants patched. This was in contract to the more luxurious lives of his wealthy cousins in Lexington. It embarrassed him to go to school with patched britches.

He also was bullied by boys at school who, because of his slightly crossed eyes, called him "cockeyed." He tried to correct his eyesight by peeping through the keyhole of a door, to strengthen his eye muscles. His eye problem added to his shyness and reserve. In later years, he lost sight in his left eye.

Robert didn't believe he shared the intimacy with his father that his younger brothers did, once saying: "My Father's life was of a kind which gave me but little opportunity to learn the details of his early career. During my childhood and early youth he was almost constantly away from home, attending courts or making political speeches.

"In 1859 when I was sixteen and when he was beginning to devote himself more to practice in his own neighbourhood, and when I would have had both the inclination and the means of gratifying my desire to become better acquainted with the history of his struggles, I went to New Hampshire to school and afterward to

Harvard College, and he became President. Henceforth any great intimacy between us became impossible. I scarcely even had ten minutes quiet talk with him during his Presidency, on account of his constant devotion to business."

While Robert and his father shared a love of the theatre, they never attended a play together. Tad, however, did sometimes go to plays with his father. One of these occasions, when an actor leading some stage soldiers was waving the American flag, he then gave it to Tad. Tad stood up and began waving the flag and sang: "We are coming, Father Abraham, three hundred thousand more, shouting the battle-cry of freedom!"

Robert, unlike Tad, never tried to endear himself to his father and seemed to disappear at moments when his father needed him. Sometimes he even appeared to deliberately annoy him, as when he did not reply to his father's telegram to "Come to Washington" after his Mother had an accident in July 1863. "Why do I hear no more of you?" Abe telegraphed him.

When the Civil War broke out, Robert's private and public status as a son of the President was complicated by his desire to enter the Army and his mother's adamant opposition to such service. Given Mary's fragile mental state, President Lincoln tended to side with her until after Robert graduated from college.

Mary Lincoln said to her husband: "Of course, Mr. Lincoln, I know that Robert's plea to go into the Army is manly and noble and I want him to go, but oh! I am so frightened he may never come back to us!"

When some White House guests criticized Robert's absence from the Army, Mrs. Lincoln said to New York Senator Ira Harris: "Robert is making his preparation now to enter the Army, Senator Harris; he is not a shirker as you seem to imply, for he has been anxious to go for a long time.

"If fault there be, it's mine, I have insisted that he should stay in college a little longer as I think an educated man can serve his country with more intelligent purpose than an ignoramus."

In January 1865, Robert left his law studies at Harvard to join the Army. His father had written General Ulysses S. Grant. Robert did not see action, but following his graduation from Harvard he served as a captain on Grant's staff in the closing days of the war. Robert was present at the courthouse in Appomattox, Virginia, when General Robert E. Lee signed the document of the Confederacy's surrender to Union. He was also present at the dedication of the Lincoln Memorial in Washington, DC. in 1922.

After the war, married Mary Eunice Harlan, the daughter of a United States Senator from Iowa, and they had three children. His only son, Abraham Lincoln II, who was nicknamed "Jack," died in France while Robert was serving as Minister in London.

The night his father was assassinated, Robert had turned down an invitation to join his parents at Ford's Theatre. He said he was fatigued after spending time in a covered wagon at a war battlefront.

After his father's death, Robert moved to an apartment in Chicago with his mother and Tad, but left after a short time. He rented his own rooms on January 1, 1866 to "begin to live with some degree of comfort," which he said he had not known when living with his parents.

Robert became a successful and wealthy lawyer and President of the Pullman Company in Chicago which built railroad cars. While he never ran for any high political office, he served the United States as the last Minister to Great Britain, before the title was changed to Ambassador, and also as Secretary of War under President Garfield.

Robert died on July 26, 1926 at his summer retreat, "Hildene," his father-in-law's mansion in Manchester, Vermont, where he had become a virtual recluse in his later years. He was described then as being "A full-fleshed man, bearded and bespectacled who was impeccable in his social relations and personal grooming." He spent much of his adult life protecting his wife and children against sensation seekers and speculators. His hobbies were astronomy and golfing.

He was the only member of his father's immediate family not to be buried in the Lincoln family plot in Springfield, Illinois. He was buried in Arlington National Cemetery in Arlington County, Virginia.

Willie Lincoln Is Born

The summer of 1850 passed into autumn, and autumn into winter. The Christmas season was coming soon and so too was the Lincolns' new baby.

Mrs. Lincoln had not been well for a month, but wanted to go to pre-holiday parties. Her doctor, her sister Elizabeth's husband, cautioned her not to and to stay home and rest. It was not an easy time for her, Abe, or Robert. Or, for that matter, Mariah and Billie. She had sent her eldest daughter, teenage Ellen, to help with preparing for some parties at the Lincoln home, but Ellen left after one day with Mrs. Lincoln.

Mary disobeyed her doctor's orders and went to Lexington to have her baby there with her parents and other relatives. However, she returned to Springfield before giving birth.

When the baby arrived on December 21, the Lincoln's named him William Wallace after the doctor. Billie Vance was disappointed. He thought the baby had been named after him.

The Lincolns always called their son "Willie," never "William," Billy," or "Bill." Abe continued to call Mariah's Billie "Bill." She said no one but he ever called her son "Bill."

As Christmas approached and Mary was back home in Springfield with the baby, Robert came to the Vance shack with presents from his parents. They were mostly clothes that Mrs. Lincoln had sewn out of things she no longer wanted to wear or Robert had outgrown. But

Mariah could see that a lot of care had gone into the sewing. Henry got some of Abe's worn shirts and bandanas. The children also got toys and store-bought candy. Mariah and Henry got two shiny new silver dollars.

Robert stayed several hours, sitting at the kitchen table and teaching both Billie and Ellen more writing. Mariah thought Ellen learned faster than Billie. Mariah learned some, too, but Henry did not seem to get it or even care for the lessons.

During the week between Christmas and New Year's, Robert came to the Vance shack almost every day to give more lessons. Each time he came, he brought some "vittles," chestnuts, and taffy that was left over from Mrs. Lincoln's holiday parties.

Mariah had never seen the Lincoln's son, Eddie, whom she referred to as a "little angel." She heard the Lincoln's say that Willie was the "spitting image" of Eddie when he was a baby.

Robert was not at home much each day, and Mariah learned why.

"They wanted to get him out of the house so he wouldn't disturb the baby or de Missy. I wanted to tell them they was makin' a mistake, but her wasn't fit to talk to, because her mind was set. She run that poor little Mastah Robert out every time he comes near. He tip-toe around like a little mouse."

Baby Willie had a habit of holding his breath, which worried both his parents.

Abe said to Mariah, "We'll have to help him over that someway, for with him holding his breath, like I have to hold my tongue, and Robert have to tip-toe, the neighbors will think the Lincoln's have moved out!"

When Mariah returned to do the Lincoln's' wash again, Robert told her, "Ma wants you, Aunt Mariah. She says she owes you an apology."

Mariah was reluctant to see Mrs. Lincoln, who was still ill after giving birth to Willie, and she did not want to disturb her, but went to her room nonetheless. The Lincoln's slept in separate bedrooms because Abe liked to read in bed, by candlelight, while Mary wanted to sleep soon as her head the pillow.

"Mariah, I owe you an apology," said Mary, and referred to past times when she had been sharp with her. "Can you find it in your heart to forgive me? I just couldn't think of starting a new year without making an effort to get your good thoughts toward me again."

Mariah recalled, "I declare I wilted plumb down like the little snow man Mastah Robert have made on the front lawn. I told de Missy I thought I was the sinna, 'stead of her. But I tole her I would forgive her so I too could start the new years right."

Mrs. Lincoln also felt guilty about Mariah having miscarried the child she was expecting before Christmas.

"If I was the cause, even indirectly, of you losing your child," said Mary, "I know God will punish me, for being so rude to you and Billie."

Mariah tried to assure her she had not been that way to them.

Mary then said she hoped Willie would bring more peace between her and Mr. Lincoln. "Now that Willie has replaced Eddie, or at least has softened the blow of dear little Eddie's going, he may come home more often and find happiness here. My only hope, so far as I'm concerned, is that my deep love for him will find a way to save our marriage."

Willie grew to be an attractive boy with light brown hair, fair skin, and blue eyes. While his younger brother Tad was more excitable and unpredictable, Willie was more quiet, amiable, cheerful, and mature for his age. His mother said he "was a very beautiful boy, with a most spiritual expression on his face," although he most often readily joined Tad in mischievous tricks and pranks. He even thought some of them up himself.

Mrs. Lincoln called Taddie her "little troublesome sunshine," while Willie was her comfort. She said he scarcely seemed a child to her. She thought they were "so unlike," yet they were "so devoted" to each other. "There love for each other was charming to behold.

Willie was both his father's and mother's favorite son. He considered himself to be "mother's boy," and resembled her more. But he also had a lot of his father in him, having many of Abe's qualities. He even held his head tilted to one side, like his father.

Mariah recalled, "Folks say that Mastah Robert war mean to Eddie and now war mean to baby Willie. I know that was not so. de Missy shoved Mastah Robert off and out, so as he wouldn't disturb. I know Mistah Abe seed it that there way too. I do know Mastah Robert wanted to hold Willie and they say he didn't know how. That wasn't no excuse. They should have teached him how. Other chillun could come in and play around Willie, but not Mastah Robert. I's not zadgeratin."

She recalled more about her favorite Lincoln son.

"That Mastah Robert was a little lonesome boy when he was at home, unless Mistah Abe war there. I think Mistah Abe should have come oftener, on Mastah Robert's account. Mistah Abe war a terrible busy man and folks say he war making heaps of money now."

Lincoln had some lucrative work as a lawyer for the Alton and Sangamon Railroad while he continued other work in private practice. He and a lawyer friend, William Herndon, were partners in a firm with an office in town.

Lincoln had become concerned when expenses had mounted because of Willie's birth and afterward. He asked her to be careful with the money he would provide from his practice and would have his partner, whom he called Bill, give her what she needed.

Mary did not like or approve of Herndon, often calling him lazy and criticizing him for drinking. She resented him thinking she spent too much. But he knew that, among other things, she bought lots of material to have new dresses made. And she bought all the bolts of the material she selected, so no other woman in town could wear a dress like hers.

Mary also criticized Abe for being away so much, at his law office or talking with friends outside the drug store in town. She said she wanted him to be home more so he could share her load in looking after the house and their children. But Abe was then away on the circuit for two months or more, never writing to her. She had more parties to make up for his absence.

When Abe returned home he learned that Mary had run up bills in local stores and charged for things he thought were unnecessary luxuries. Mariah said they often quarreled about money matters.

Robert left the house when they quarreled, and went to the barn. He and some new friends made a theater, with boxes to sit on, and made a stage curtain from material he found in the house.

Abe entered the barn and Robert pleaded with him, to take him and his friends to the woods so they could climb trees. He said he would, soon, then began hanging from a rafter by some rope and swung himself around. Robert and his friends watched as he did a trick called "skin-the-cat," hanging upside-down.

After a while, Abe couldn't untangle himself, so Robert ran into the kitchen in the house and asked Mariah to get the meat cleaver and go to the barn with him. All his time, Mary was upstairs in her bedroom nursing another headache.

"When I git there, Mistah Abe war hangin' by the feet and head, all tangle up."

She got him free and Abe, Robert, and the other boys all laughed. Abe then told the boys not to go into the house so they would not disturb his ailing wife, and promised to take them all to the woods when he returned from the circuit.

Mariah returned home later that day and told Henry about the skin-the-cat adventure. Billie looked mad, because his Ma had not taken him along that day and he missed out on all the fun with Mastah Robert.

Pranks of Willie and Tad

Tad and Willie were always running around and making noise in the house. They were constantly playing tricks and pranks on their parents, Mariah, and visitors. Often, they tied the strings of their mother's apron to the chair she was sitting in, causing her to almost fall when she stood up. That was one of their more innocent pranks.

A neighbor woman who lived in a house across the street from the Lincoln's said, "One evening Mr. and Mrs. Lincoln were to attend a reception at the home of Mr. Dubois, the state auditor, a couple of blocks down on Eighth street. My mother was helping Mrs. Lincoln dress for the party. Willie and Tad came home from a candy-pull. They were smeared with molasses candy from head to foot.

"When they heard of the party, they wanted to go, too. Robert, who at that time was planning to enter Harvard, was to stay at home with the little boys. Mrs. Lincoln said firmly that they could not go, whereupon the two boys set up a cry. Their mother was steadfast, and the boys were determined. They were kicking and screaming when Mr. Lincoln entered.

"'This will never do,'" he said. "'Mary, if you will let the boys go, I will take care of them.'

"'Why, Father, you know that is no place for boys to be. When people give a party like that it is no place children.' By this time the boys began to listen.

"'But.'" said Mr. Lincoln, "'I will take them around the back way, and they can stay in the kitchen.' He then talked to the boys about being good and making no promises that were not to be kept, and it was arranged that the boys should go if Robert and my mother should get them dressed. They were cleaned up, and in the haste Tad found his short trousers on hind-side before.

"At this he set up another storm, because he 'couldn't walk good,' which his father quieted by a wave of his hand and saying, 'Remember, now, remember.'

"When the little boys were ready, they went ahead with their father, not to the kitchen but to the full reception. With Robert, Mrs. Lincoln followed in, in a beautiful canary-colored satin dress, low neck and short sleeves, and large hoop-skirts, after the manner of the time."

Abe was a lot more tolerant of his young sons' antics than friends and guests in their home. Don Piatt, an Ohio newspaperman, recalled one night having dinner in the Lincoln's home in the autumn of 1860. As they sat in the parlor, "... all the while, two little boys, his sons, clambered over those legs, patted his cheeks, pulled his nose, and poked their fingers in his eyes, without causing reprimand or even notice."

Mary was nowhere near as patient with the boys as was Abe. A Springfield neighbor, Anna Eastman, recalled looking out her kitchen window one summer day when she witnessed a scene in the Lincoln's kitchen. Mrs. Lincoln was berating her son Tad for not giving her back a dime in change after going to the store. Tad denied that he had used the money on himself and claimed that he had lost it. His mother accused him of being a "bad boy" and a "thief" and got a switch which she turned on Tad's legs.

At that point, Mr. Lincoln came in the kitchen and asked Mrs. Lincoln, "What does this mean?" After she gave her interpretation of events, he asked "are you sure?" He ordered Tad to turn out his pockets, from which a dime dropped. At that point, according to Anna many years later, "occurred what I shall never forget, for Mr. Lincoln turned to his wife and literally looked down on her, because he was so tall, and said in a voice gentle and tender with understanding: 'Mary! Mary!' That was all he said, and his wife made no reply."

Willie and Tad attended Miss Corcoran's school in Springfield. Abe did not want Tad to be "pushed in his schooling," because of his speech impediment and learning disabilities. As a result of this leniency, Tad often skipped school to play and developed a "distaste for books." When he lost his baby teeth, his second teeth came in crooked, adding to the teasing he got from classmates.

Lincoln's aide John Hay said "the two little boys, aged eight [*Tad*] and ten [*Willie*] kept the house in an uproar with their playing and pranks. They drove their tutor wild with their good-natured disobedience; they organized a minstrel show in the attic. William was, with all his boyish frolic, a child of great promise, a boy capable of close application.

Tad had a fancy for drawing up railway time tables, and would conduct an imaginary train from Chicago to New York with perfect precision. He wrote childish verses, which sometimes attained the unmerited honors of print."

Willie was both precocious and engaging, his personality and his mind were both advanced. One relative described Willie as "a noble, beautiful boy, of great mental activity, unusual intelligence, wonderful memory, methodical, frank and loving, a counterpart of his father, save that he was handsome."

Springfield photographer J. G. Stewart recalled that Willie "was the brainiest boy I ever saw. His memory was so great that after he had heard a sermon he could repeat it almost word for word."

Childhood friend Fred T. Dubois, recalled that Willie "was very studious and took delight in discussing the problems of the day with the other boys."

Willie liked to read and his interior life mirrored that of the President. He shared his father's thoughtfulness and his father's sense of humor. He also shared his father's ability to put people at ease and his father's interest in history, as well as his father's early attempts at poetry.

Willie and his father seemed to share a similar inner life, separate from the rest of the Lincoln family. Willie shared his father's deliberative thought processes.

As Mr. Lincoln observed his son thinking at the breakfast table one morning, he told a visiting congressman: "I know every step of the process by which that boy arrived at his satisfactory solution of the question before him, as it is by just such slow methods I attain results."

Willie's mother called him "the idolized child of the household."

Back in Springfield, Willie was a precocious politician who used to stand on the terrace of their house and urge passer-by to "Vote for Old Abe." He was a pretty good speech-maker himself, and his boy companions, at the end of their parades, would call for a speech from Willie' to which he would proudly respond.

Willie, like his brothers, could be persistent. One friend recalled Willie coming into his father's office in the summer of 1860. "Father I want twenty-five cents," said Willie. "My son," said Mr. Lincoln, "What do you want of twenty-five centers?" Willie responded, "I want it to buy candy with." To which Mr. Lincoln said, "My son, I shall not give you twenty-five centers, but will give you five cents."

He put the five-cent piece on his desk, but Willie turned away and left the office. Mr. Lincoln told his companion that Willie "… will be back after that in a few moments…as soon as he finds I will give him no more he will come and get it." Sure enough, Willie snuck back in quietly, retrieved his money and departed "without saying a word."

Lincoln family biographer Ruth Painter Randall wrote: "The two younger boys were so devoted to each other it was almost as hard for Willie to witness Tad's tears as it was for Mr. Lincoln. He looked on sorrowfully at their father's failure to bring Tad out of his woe, then lapsed into an absorbed silence which lasted for ten or fifteen minutes.

He was evidently trying hard to think of some way he could cheer Tad up. Mr. Lincoln was watching Willie and making sure that no one disturbed his mental concentration. Finally Willie clasped both hands together, shut his teeth over his lower lip, and looked up into his father's face with a smile. Mr. Lincoln had been waiting for this.

"There!" Abe exclaimed. "You have it now, my boy, have you not?" Then turning to a guest who was at the breakfast table he explained, "Know every step of the process by which that boy arrived at his satisfactory solution of the question before him, as it by just such slow methods I attain results."

Tad made a mess of the paints with which portrait artist Thomas Hicks had set out to work on a painting of Abe in the spring of 1860, a few months before being elected President.

Hicks recalled, "My color tubes were on a table at the side of the room. One day Mr. Lincoln's little son, Tad, with a companion, came noiselessly into the office. His father was sitting at his desk with his back to them, and so absorbed that he did not hear them come in. I was busy with the portrait.

"The little fellows got among my paints. They took the brightest blue, yellow and red. Then they squeezed from a tube, into their little palms, a lot of the red, and smeared it on the wall; then they took the blue and smeared that in another place, and afterward they smeared the yellow. I saw their excitement and mischief from the beginning, but held my peace and enjoyed watching the enthusiastic young colorists, as they made their first effort in brilliant wall decoration, while, getting the paint all over their hands, their faces and their clothes, the little fellows were as still as mice.

"At this juncture of affairs, Tad's father turned in his chair and saw their condition and what they had done. He said, in the mildest tone and with the greatest affection, 'Boys! boys! You mustn't meddle with Mr. Hicks's paints; now run home and have your faces and hands washed;' and the little fellows took his advice and left the office without a word."

Willie and Tad tended to get sick together, apparently because they spent so much time together and enjoyed the same things such as books and toys.

Both came down with measles in the White House shortly after President Lincoln was inaugurated in March 1861. In February 1862, both again got sick -- this time apparently with typhoid fever.

During Willie's illness, according to William O. Stoddard, "there is an increasingly gloomy shadow in the house. Work in all the rooms goes on as usual, but now and then the President rises nervously from his chair by the desk and window, walks hastily out of his office and over into the family side of the building. He will not stop to speak to any one by the way, and he is never gone long. He is a bondsman, and he cannot spare many of the moments scared to the work of saving the life of the Republic, not even to linger over the pallid face of his sick boy. He must look at him and come away."

After Willie's death, wrote John Hay, the President's "bereaved heart seemed ...to pour out its fullness on his youngest child."

"Quick in mind, and impulse, like his mother, with her naturally sunny temperament, he [*Tad*] was the life, as also the worry of the household," wrote Elizabeth Todd Grimsley.

Like his father, Tad was energized by people. Life was a drama in which Tad sought to cast as many people as possible as his sidekicks. His heart was as big as his father's and he befriended all White House visitors except the stuffy and the self-important, who thought he was altogether undisciplined.

More attractive to Tad were those who sought his father's favors, whom aide William O. Stoddard recalled "were quick to seize upon what seemed so vulnerable a point as Mr. Lincoln's affection for his boy, and attempt to bring themselves to the favorable notice of the all powerful President by the assiduity with which they cultivated his little pet.

"Of course they succeeded with Tad, for a boy's heart is easily fished for, and there were a few of the earlier approaches on this line which were tolerably successful; but only a very few found their way to his knee or table before Mr. Lincoln saw the point, and 'Tad's

---

clients' became more a matter for joke than anything else. Otherwise, as a general rule, it was not apt to be to any man's advantage to have his case pressed by a member of the President's family."

Journalist Noah Brooks frequently visited the White House and wrote that Tad "was the irrepressible spirit of fun and mischief which, through the whole of his father's term, gave the life in the White House its only comic element. This lad, the complete embodiment of animal spirits, may be called one of the historic boys of America. His name is closely identified with that of his father in the minds of all who were admitted to the inner precincts of the White House; and thousands who never saw the home apartments of that gloomy building knew the tricky spirit that brightened the weary years which Lincoln passed in Washington."

Although he annoyed "serious" people, Tad was a special favorite with soldiers and he delighted in visiting them with his father. Noah Brooks recalled one such visit when the family visited "the Army of the Potomac…and although he was greatly delighted with the bustle, animation, and brilliancy of the reviews during those memorable days, he was anxious for home when night and darkness came and there was nothing to engage his restless mind. Then he would begin to coax his father to go back to Washington.

"The President, although slightly annoyed by the boy's persistence, apologized for him, saying that there was a new pony at home waiting to be tried under the saddle by Tad, who had finally compassed a darling project of his own. Finally, to bribe the lad to cease his importunities, Lincoln offered to give him a dollar if he would not pester him with further inquiries about going home.

"The boy accepted the bargain, but he did not keep his agreement very well; and on the last day of our stay he shyly reminded his father that he needed that dollar very much. Lincoln thoughtfully took out of his pocket-book a dollar bill, and looking in the boy's eyes, said: 'Now, Taddie, my son, do you think you have earned this?' The lad hung his head, and answered not a word. 'Well, my son,' said the indulgent father, 'although I don't think you have kept your part of the bargain, I will keep mine, and you cannot reproach me with breaking faith, anyway.'"

Mrs. Lincoln's cousin, Elizabeth Grimsley, recalled: "One morning, Mr. Lincoln coming in to a late breakfast…found his 'little man' dissolved in tears, a sight he could never serenely bear, and at once set about to discover the trouble. 'Why! Father, such ungrateful soldiers! When I gave them tracts, and asked them to read them, they laughed loud at me, and said they had plenty of paper to start fires with, and would rather have a posey." His father took him in his arms, pressed him tightly to him, kissed him, and tried to console him, but it was days before the men saw their little friend's laughing face again, as he could not readily forgive ridicule."

Tad could not abide breaking faith with his soldiers, When one soldier yelled to the President to "send along the greenbacks, he asked what the soldier meant. When "told that the army had not been paid for some time, on account of the scarcity of greenbacks, he said, with some indignation, 'Why doesn't Governor [*Salmon P.*] Chase print 'em some, then?'"

Despite his lack of academic preparation, noted Noah Brooks, "Tad comprehended many practical realities that are far beyond the grasp of most boys. Even when he could scarcely read, he knew much about the cost of things, the details of trade, the principles of mechanics, and the habits of animals, all of which showed the activity of his mind and the odd turn of his thoughts.

"His father took great interest in everything that concerned Tad, and when the long day's work was done, and the little chap had related to the President all that had moved him or had taken up his attention during the daylight hours, and had finally fallen asleep under a drowsy cross-examination, the weary father would turn once more to his desk and work on into the night, for his cares never ended. Then, shouldering the sleeping child, the man for whom millions of good men and women nightly prayed took his way through the silent corridors and passage to his boy's bedchamber."

One account of Tad at the time of Abe's assassination had him at a theatre watching a play when the news was shouted that Lincoln had been shot. However, another account said that Tad did not know of the tragedy until later the day Abe died, when his mother told him the tragic news.

The Rev. Phineas Gurley recalled that Tad was distraught over his father's death and exclaimed: "O what shall I do? What shall I do? My Brother is dead. My Father is dead. O what shall I do? What will become of me? O what shall I do? O mother you will not die will you? O don't you die Ma. You won't die will you Mother? If you die I shall be all alone. O don't die Ma." Even Dr. Gurley broke down at that point.

In the years after his father's death, Tad matured socially and academically. His father's attitude had been: "Let him run; there's time enough yet for him to learn his letters. Bob was just such a little rascal and now he is a very decent boy."

John Hay wrote: "Although still a mere child at the death of his father, this terrible shock greatly sobered and steadied him. His brother Robert at once took charge of his education, and he made rapid progress up to the time of his sailing for Europe with his mother. He has ever since remained with her, displaying a thoughtful devotion and tenderness beyond his years, and strangely at variance with the mischievous thoughtlessness of his childhood. He came back a short while ago, greatly improved by his residence abroad, but always the same cordial, frank, warm-hearted boy."

Willie and Tad played even more jokes and pranks when they began living in the White House. It was much larger than their home in Springfield so there was more room for their antics, and a house full of servants to torment.

Soon after moving into the White House they became good friends two boys their age and a sister a few year older. They were the children of Judge and Mrs. Horatio Nelson Taft: "Bud" who was a year older than Willie, and "Holly," about the same age as Tad. Their sister Julia was sixteen, too old to join in the fun.

Willie and Bud bonded partly because they were both somewhat more restrained in their antics than were Tad and his pal Holly. This included the younger boys taking Tad's toy cannon and exploding it in a room where the President was conferring with his Cabinet about the

Civil War. Some of those present thought the Confederates were shelling the building. Lincoln knew better and just laughed.

One morning, after the Taft boys had spent the night in the White House, Tad and Holly disappeared after breakfast. While Willie and Bud played on the flat White House roof, Tad and Holly were still missing in the afternoon. An anxious Mrs. Lincoln had staff search all over for them, but to no avail. After dark, a man brought them back in his carriage.

When asked where they had gone, Tad said they had gone into the city to explore. As dinnertime approached, "A man who knew Pa gave us some dinner in the restaurant."

The boys then had gone farther into the city and, as Tad said, "We went down steps pretty near to China." They then got lost and found themselves in an "awful dark" place with rats. They called for help and a man heard, rescued them, and brought them to the White House.

The White House gardener once complained that Tad had picked all of the strawberries in the garden that had been intended for dessert at a formal dinner.

Willie and Tad attended Presbyterian church services with their parents and also went to Sunday School. Willie took Sunday School more seriously because he indicated that he wanted to be a preacher when he grew up. Tad also took church services more as another place to play. He often sat on the floor of the pew and played with whatever he had in his pockets.

When Tad asked why he should go to such a solemn thing as Sunday School, Abe replied, "Every educated person should know something about the *Bible* and the *Bible* stories."

The attic held a special fascination for the Lincoln brothers and their new playmates. Willie and Tad missed the snows of winter in Springfield, so they improvised a snow storm in the attic. They and their pals made a sled out of some barrel staves and an old chair and tore up handfuls of greeting cards with the names of famous people and tore them up to pretend they were snowflakes falling.

One day, the boys decided to put on a show in the attic. Besides the Lincoln and Taft brothers, there were a few others of their boy friends. They charged five cents admission to White House staff and anyone else who came. They performed in black face, using shoe polish and burnt cork.

Willie and Bud put on dresses belonging to Mrs. Lincoln, enlisting the reluctant help of Julia.

The patriotic show opened with all of the boys singing "Hail Columbia," followed by Tad and another boy, Billy Sanders, singing "The Star-Spangled Banner." Bud Taft and Joe Corkhead then showed Union solidarity by singing "Dixie Land." Willie, dressed as a Southern belle, sang "Home Sweet Home."

Pranks were temporarily suspended in March when both Willie and Tad came down with measles. Soon after their recovery they noticed that the streets were full of soldiers to fight in the expected Civil War. They began going with their parents to Army camps and watched as parades passed in front of the White House.

One of Tad's pranks was not very funny, except to him. He loved the uniforms of one particular unit that joined the North in the Civil War. They were worn by the American Zouaves, similar to those of the French Zouaves who had fought in the Crimean War (1853-1856). It was an European conflict regarding the safety and rights of Christian minorities in the Holy Land which was controlled by the Turkish Ottoman Empire.

The American version of the French Zouave uniform consisted of a bright red cap with gold braid, brass buttons on the red tunic, a grey jacket with a red sash, and loose-fitting grey pantaloons. Zouaves carried a sword, a very heavy revolver, and a large and very sharp Bowie knife. When Tad lived in the White House, he had Jack, his toy Union soldier, dressed as a Zouave.

The Zouaves came into Tad's life in Springfield when a young man named Elmer Ellsworth came to town wearing the flashy uniform. He organized the American Zouaves in Springfield while studying law in the Lincoln law offices. Tad and Willie both took to him right away, climbing all over him. Their parents also liked him very much and regarded him almost as another son.

When the boys came down with the measles, they passed a severe case of the child's disease on to Ellsworth. They all recovered.

Ellsworth's Zouaves in America began as merely a ceremonial contingent at parades. In the middle of April, 1861, when the nation was in civil war, the Zouaves joined the action on the side of the Union. Ellsworth held the rank of colonel.

On May 24, Ellsworth and a few of his company went to a hotel in Alexandria, Virginia, where a Confederate flag was flying on the roof. After taking down the flag with his own hands, the owner of the hotel shot him dead, then was shot and killed by one of the gallant young colonel's men. Willie and Tad were sorely grieved over the death of their favorite Zouave, as were their parents. Lincoln wept at Ellsworth's funeral in the East Room of the White House.

One day, Tad found the Confederate flag that had cost Ellsworth his life. It had been given to his mother. During a parade to celebrate a Union battle victory, he took the flag and stood it in front of the Taft home. It was his idea of a joke, but was a very poor one and he was reprimanded.

Tad did not learn his lesson and went a giant step farther with the Confederate flag. When Lincoln was viewing another parade in front of the White House while holding a Union flag to honor the marching troops. Tad came up behind him, waving the Confederate flag. Lincoln was mortified but did not scold Tad. He merely took him and the flag into his arms and turned them over to an orderly who carried them away.

In June, Willie and Tad raised a company of boy soldiers and called them "Mrs. Lincoln's Zouaves." Only Willie and Tad wore the red, blue, and gold uniform of their favorite soldiers. Willie was a colonel, Bud Taft a major, Holly a captain, and Tad was the drum major, making as much noise as he could at their parades in and around the White House.

The Circus Comes to Town

Mariah's recollections skipped to 1855 and 1856. Lincoln ran for the U.S. Senate in February 1855 but was defeated by a vote of the Illinois Legislature and returned to private law practice.

In the spring of 1855, Tad became ill and almost died of a lung infection and a high fever. Mariah said that Doctor Wallace worked night and day to save him, and the boy recovered. After Abe left home to go on the circuit again, Willie developed weak lungs. Mary was able to contact Abe and he returned home to help her care for him and he soon recovered.

Mary decided to have a sewing a party for ladies of her church. The party would consist of them sewing clothes for the church's missionary work. She put the boys' playthings in the shed to clear the house for the party, and set up a stage and seats in the barn for a play. While she and the other ladies sewed, Willie and Tad and some of their pals would have cake and candy and lemonade in the barn. Willie was then about four and a half years old, and Tad was three. Robert was twelve, and would be in school the day of the party.

While the ladies sewed in the parlor, a regular circus came to the Lincoln home.

Said Mariah, "The sewing was over, as well as the gossip about those who warn't there. Then the serving begin [*snacks and lemonade*]. In march Willie and Tad and that whole kitten posy of boys. Each one have an animal.

Willie first let down the white rat on the floor. The women put up their feet and scream. Some even stand on their chair.

"Then up step a boy with a turtle. Some kittens come next. A whole slew of chicks, one from each boy. A hop toad, a big bull frog croaking for to go back to the water. An old hen, and the crow that repeat over and over, 'Get out, ya bums!' The boys have taught him that.

"At last, some boys let down on the floor the big tom cat. The womans screamin' scare that black debil and I never seen such racing 'round in a house in my born days. The womans put for the door, grab their umbrellas and coats and they depart screamin' at their kids to come or they would beat the daylights out of them.

"De Missy war humiliate. Her grab Willie and scream, 'Why did you do such a thing to me?'

"Little Taddie like it so much, he roll and roll on the floor and clap his little hands. I bet that war the best party those boys ever have."

Mrs. Lincoln wailed again, "Why did you do it?"

Mariah said Willie replied, "We got tired so we decided to have a circus parade and let the animals act. We wanted the ladies to see our show. I was to bring in the chariot driven by the white rat. Each animal was to have an act, but they acted better than we taught them. Jim Crow was the clown. He was to say, 'Get out, you bums!' just as the circus clown said in the circus you took us to. You remember that, don't you, Ma?'"

"De Missy didn't answer," said Mariah. "She war too mad. Then Willie say, "'Well, Pa will laugh. He don't like a gang of women here all the time anyway.' Her eyes spat fire and her yell, 'William Wallace, did your father say that?'

"Willie war smart. He grin and say, 'No, Ma. But I can tell when Pa doesn't like a thing. He's sad and quiet. But I bet he'd of liked our circus.'"

Mariah then recalled, "Sure enough, when Mistah Abe come home and de Missy tell him all 'bout the fracas the boys have raise, he in his high-pitched voice say, 'Good!'"

A black serving girl, Emilie, whom Mary had hired to help with the sewing party was still there and said to Abe: "Brother Abram, you missed the biggest show of your life. Why can't we have another party soon, when you are home, and have the boys put on their circus parade again?"

Abe replied, "Little sister, I do believe I'm in on that party, if I have to miss the circuit. I'll never again tell a story that tops that one."

Abe, the boys, and Emilie all laughed and Mary Lincoln ran upstairs.

"For days after that," Mariah remembered, "Mistah Abe would bust out laughing, if Willie or Taddie war near. They would always say, 'Pa, when can we have the circus?'

"He would pat and hug them. Then he would run for some of the animals. The chicks, white rat, and the crow climb all over that man with them two boys pesterin, even when he read. He would join in the fun with them."

When Robert came home from school later that afternoon, his brothers told him all about their circus parade and he got a good laugh out of hearing about it.

Mariah said she thought the boys liked their father the most. She recalled, "They never stop to think, their pa could 'preciate them more, 'cause he war not with them that much. But their Ma sewed, cooked, sometime washed.

Nursed 'em, kept a nice home for 'em, kept 'em clean. Took them to shows and church, waited on them when sick, and welcome their friends. Even if her warn't much fun, her never abuse them and did the best in the world for 'em, as her see it."

Willie was six in 1856 and it was time for him to begin going to school. Abe wanted his favorite son not only to get a good education, he wanted him to be taught the things that built character and would make him a fine person. He wrote to his teacher the following letter:

My son starts school today. It is all going to be strange and new to him for a while and I wish you would treat him gently. It is an adventure that might take him across continents. All adventures that probably include wars, tragedy and sorrow. To live this life will require faith, love and courage.

So dear Teacher, will you please take him by his hand and teach him things he will have to know, teaching him – but gently, if you can. Teach him that for every enemy, there is a friend. He will have to know that all men are not just, that all men are not true. But teach him also that for every scoundrel there is a hero, that for every crooked politician, there is a dedicated leader.

Teach him if you can that 10 cents earned is of far more value than a dollar found. In school, teacher, it is far more honorable to fail than to cheat. Teach him to learn how to gracefully lose, and enjoy winning when he does win.

Teach him to be gentle with people, tough with tough people. Steer him away from envy if you can and teach him the secret of quiet laughter. Teach him if you can – how to laugh when he is sad, teach him there is no shame in tears. Teach him there can be glory in failure and despair in success. Teach him to scoff at cynics.

Teach him if you can the wonders of books, but also give time to ponder the extreme mystery of birds in the sky, bees in the sun and flowers on a green hill. Teach him to have faith in his own ideas, even if every one tell him they are wrong.

Try to give my son the strength not to follow the crowd when everyone else is doing it. Teach him to listen to every one, but teach him also to filter all that he hears on a screen of truth and take only the good that comes through.

Teach him to sell his talents and brains to the highest bidder but never to put a price tag on his heart and soul. Let him have the courage to be impatient, let him have the patient to be brave. Teach him to have sublime faith in himself, because then he will always have sublime faith in mankind, in God.

This is the order, teacher, but see what best you can do. He is such a nice little boy and he is my son.

Goats, Ponies, and a Turkey

As much as Abraham Lincoln loved animals, and the stories about that are many and well-documented, his sons Willie and Tad may even have loved them more, especially the youngest, Tad.

Among the many gifts the boys received when they lived in the White House were a pony for each and two goats. The goats were named "Nanny" and "Nanko" and Abe gave them the run of the executive mansion. Mrs. Lincoln did not like that much but allowed it because both she and Abe spoiled their young sons and let them have and do most anything and everything.

The White House staff often complained that the goats were wrecking the first floor, where they roamed freely and damaged furniture and plants. Abe ignored all that and told them, the goat "interests the boys and does hem good; let the goats be." He also was reported to have taken pride in the goats' affection for him.

Willie and Tad hitched the goats to carts or kitchen chairs and drove them through the main floor of the White House. One time, Tad harnessed Nanko to a chair and drove through the East Room during a reception. Dignified women raised up their hoop skirts as Tad drove around the room and out the door again. Lincoln sometimes played with his sons and the goats on the grounds of the White House.

Nanko got out once and dug up the flower bulbs that had been planted by White House gardener John Watt.

Nanny was taken to the Soldiers' Home but caused such destruction to the flowers that she was returned to the White House. Another day, she was found lying in the middle of Tad's bed, chewing her cud.

Elizabeth Keckley said one day Abe told her: "Come here and look at my two goats. I believe they are the kindest and best goats in the world. See how they sniff the clear air, and skip and play in the sunshine. Whew! What a jump!," he exclaimed as one of the goats made a lofty spring. "Madam Elizabeth, did you ever before see such an active goat?"

Tad Saves a Turkey's Life

One of the most often told stories about Tad and his love for animals was the one in which he had his father spare the life of a turkey who had been sentenced to death for a Christmas season dinner.

Late in 1863, a live turkey was sent to the White House for the Lincoln's to feast on during the holidays.

Tad, then age 10, took an instant liking to the turkey and befriended the bird. He had it follow him around the White House grounds and named it Jack, feeding it as a pet.

When it neared time for Jack to be prepared for the Lincoln's Christmas dinner, Tad burst into one of his father's Cabinet meetings. He cried loudly that Jack was about to be killed. He said he had obtained a temporary delay from the "executioner" so he could put Jack's case before the President to have the bird pardoned.

"Jack should not be killed," implored Tad. "It is wicked."

Abe replied, "Jack was sent here to be killed and eaten. I can't help it."

Tad persisted, sobbing: "He's a good turkey, and I don't want him killed."

Lincoln paused in the midst of the Cabinet meeting and took out a card. On it, he wrote an order of reprieve. Jack's life was to be spared.

Tad raced back out of the room waving the pardon over his head and ran to show it to the "executioner." He had saved Jack's life just in time.

Another story about Jack the turkey took place when Abraham Lincoln was running for a second term as President. On Tuesday, November 8, 1864 a special polling place had been set up on the grounds of the White House especially for soldiers who chose to vote. Jack the turkey strutted in front of some of the soldiers and broke in line. Lincoln saw this and looked at Tad. He asked whether Jack should vote, and Tad replied, "He is under age."

Jack the turkey is said to have reminded Abe of when he was a boy of about eight. His father was not at home, so Abe asked his mother, Nancy Hanks Lincoln, if he might use his father's gun to shoot at a flock of wild turkeys. She gave her permission and he reportedly shot and killed one of the birds. But when he saw the bird dead, he vowed that he would never again "pull the trigger on any larger game." He felt deeply sorrowful that he had ended the life of such a beautiful bird.

The story of Tad saving the life of a Christmas turkey has had a long ripple effect. In the years that followed, President Bill Clinton reportedly spared the life of a 60-pound turkey named "Willis," and President George W.II. Bush pardoned two turkeys named "Pumpkin" and "Pecan." In 2008, President Barack Obama granted pardons to two 45-pound turkeys named "Courage" and "Carolina." In 2010 he similarly spared the lives of two more 45-pound turkeys, "Apple" and "Cider;" in 2011 he pardoned two more turkeys, "Liberty" and "Peace;" two more in 2012 called "Cobbler" and

"Gobbler;" in 2013 turkeys named "Popcorn" and "Caramel;" and in 2014 he pardoned "Mac" and "Cheese," and in 2015 he pardoned "Honest" and "Abe."

By far Abraham Lincoln's dog, Fido, a mutt, was said to be his favorite pet. Fido was a floppy-eared, rough-coated, yellowish dog of uncertain ancestry but probably with some German Shepherd and Labrador Retriever in his mix. He had been by Abe's side from when he was a prairie lawyer through to his Presidency in the White House. Sometimes, Fido carried bundles of letters from the post office in his mouth as he and his master walked the streets of Springfield.

Fido often accompanied Abe on walks to the local market in Springfield, trailing behind carrying a parcel in his mouth. Lincoln would sometimes stop at the barber shop for a haircut, and Fido would wait outside with other customers' pets. Fido was a dog who loved attention and when bored, would spend many minutes chasing his own tail.

In early 1861, as Abe prepared to leave his home in Springfield to become President, he faced many momentous tasks, but none he dreaded more than telling his two youngest sons, Willie and Tad, that the family's beloved pet dog, Fido, would not be accompanying them to Washington. Lincoln was afraid the skittish mutt couldn't endure the long train ride, and also had known that Fido was terrified at noises such as from train whistles and clanging church bells and cannon fire that had announced his presidential nomination. He very reluctantly decided to leave Fido behind with two of his sons' playmates, John and Frank Roll. They promised to take good care of him. Their father was a carpenter who had earlier remodeled the Lincoln house.

Abe asked the Roll family never to scold Fido for entering he house with muddy paws. He was not to be tied up alone in the backyard. He also was to be allowed into the Roll home whenever he scratched at the door, and into the family's dining room at meal times. The Lincoln's had allowed Fido to be given food by everyone sitting around the table.

To make Fido feel at home, Abe gave the Rolls their horsehair sofa that the dog liked to nap on.

Abe's horse, Old Bob, also had been left behind in Springfield when the Lincoln's moved to Washington. After the assassination in 1865, Old Bob walked behind the hearse in the funeral procession in Springfield, wearing a mourning jacket with silver fringe.'

John Roll brought Fido back to his original home to meet the mourners who had gathered there.

Sadly, less than a year later, Fido also was assassinated, by a man who killed him while drunk.

Right and Wrong

Mariah Vance recalled that in November, 1858, Abe Lincoln was at home preparing to talk politics with some Republican Parry leaders in Springfield. Shortly before they would arrive, he sat in his bedroom and soaked his feet in a tub of water. He suffered from corns and bunions, and had a case of frostbite.

Mariah was in the house to serve sandwiches and tea to the visiting politicians.

"There war lots of work upstairs I have to do after my kitchen work," Mariah recalled. "When I got upstairs, there war Mistah Abe and the two boys right there in my way. [*Willie was then almost eight, and Tad about five.*] The boys tearin' 'round as always, and Mistah Abe with his two poor big feet in the water. He carry the water upstairs from the pump in the back yard. He washed and soaked his feet in cold water summer and winter.

"Mistah Abe call to the boys. They go to their Pa on a gallop. He say, 'Keep out of Aunt Mariah's way.'

"Just then, Taddie spy a picture he never see before, on the tub. He and Willie both squat to look at all those pictures on that tin foot-tub. Seems like they never could get 'nough lookin' at those pictures."

Mariah then told how that political party went.

"On this day of the biggest party, when about the whole of Springfield would come in their carriages with their finery on, I was working so fast I was all out of breath upstairs and de Missy war workin' hard too. In midst of all this hub-bub, in come a bunch of men down in front.

"De Missy war just then 'rangin' the dinin' room table after dustin' and 'rangin' the furniture, and couldn't go to the door. I sure was a mess, from top of my haid to my feet. So Mistah Abe pull his feet out of the tub. He give them a wipe, put on his carpet slippers, and go down and let that mob in.

"He take their hats and hang them on the hall tree, then led them into the parlor that war only about half done clean. He say, 'Be seated, gentlemen,' and then they give to talk.

"There war de Missy, caged for a full half-hour in the kitchen. Mistah Abe call her, then go back to look for her to 'troduce to the gang of those men in the parlor. Not seein' her, he say, all jokin,' "'I suppose Mrs. Lincoln is out mussing up something so she can find something to straighten up. That little woman is the busiest little body in the world.' The men laugh at that.

"I war doin' my best to keep those boys quiet upstairs. I say do this and do that, to help. When I say, 'Your Pa have left that tub right in my way.' I sure start a hullabaloo, but I still didn't stop gabbin' to them boys. 'Your Pa always throw the water out of the upstairs window. He can throw it far enough it done didn' drip down the house.'

"I tole the boys I'd made them johnny-cakes with maple syrup they like, if they be quiet and not scatter trash about faster than I could clean. [*Johnny-cakes were like small pancakes, flatbread made out of white ground cornmeal, water or milk, and sugar.*]

"When they got too quiet, I have to see what was up. Sure 'nough, those two war workin' like little scamps that they was pullin' that foot tub. They say so it be out of my way. I say, 'You is good boys to help Aunt Mariah.'

"They war whisperin.' I thought it war 'cause I ask them to be quiet. Right there I say those two little angels is being good for johnny-cake.

"In less than a shake, I hear that foot tub tumble down those stairs. I run to see.

"'Holy Gawd!' I say. Those boys bust out so loud laughin.' With noise of that tumblin' tub, Mistah Abe and de Missy come tearin.'

The tub had been full of water upstairs, and now water was all over the stairs and onto the parlor floor in a small flood.

"Mistah Abe take one look in that parlor. He excuse himself to the men and say, 'I have a little job to take care of for a second.' De Missy war wringin' her hands. Mistah Abe tell her, 'Mother, it's nothing much to worry about.' But he put his hand over her mouth, for fear her would rant and scream.

"Then he pick up that foot-tub, put Taddie in it. He stood up and hug his Pa around the neck. Mistah Abe put his arm around de Missy. He knewed that was the way to quiet her, if he made a little love to her.

"That other rowdy, Willie, follow with his Pa and Ma and Taddie, out to the shed where Mistah Abe lock the boys in with Jim Crow and the other pets and pests. He kiss de Missy and pat her. Her war fit to be tied, but then he come back laughin.'

"When he ask the boys why he do it, they say, 'Well, Pa, besides helping Aunt Mariah by getting that tub of water out of her way, we remembered you told us about Niagara Falls and the cat-racks [*cataracts. Abe and Mary had visited Niagara Falls in July, 1857*]. That made us want to make the cat-racks. That tub was just the boat bouncing on the rocks going over the Falls.'

"Mistah Abe say, 'Well, boys, you got the right idea, but in the wrong place.' And as always, he laugh split to kill.

"But those stairs was sure a big mess to clean and dry, with all the pile of other work for the party. All Mastah Abe say war, 'Well, that's one way of cleaning the stairs and carpet in short order.'"

Mariah said Abe never left his foot-tub of water standing again. Mrs. Lincoln said that was another example he would have to set for his children to follow. She did not think the politicians who were in the house had any idea of what had happened or why. After their meeting and they had left, Abe went back to the shed to let the boys out.

"No whippin;, no scoldin,'" said Mariah. "No do this or do that. But there they was, perched on his shoulders, laughing like they war on one of those new-fangled merry-go-rounds. Jim Crow war screamin' to them, 'Come back, come back!' That crow missed them when they out of its sight, like it was its lost brother."

Mariah then told about the whole family's love for cats.

"They have cats of all colors and kinds. Little kitty baby ones nursing their Mammy cats, and big toms. De Missy wouldn't have them in the house, so they have to stay in the shed or the barn.

"One day, the boys decide to take the Mammy cat and some suckin' baby kitty for a trip to see their brother, Robert, who was in school then. They say those cats need educatin,' too.

"They hitch two toms to the tongue of the wagon. Willie hold the so they couldn't start off 'til Taddie put the mother cat and babies in. Then Willie start to lead those two tom cats. 'Bout that time, Taddie 'cided they have better go faster or they won't get to school that day. So he give that wagon a push from the hind side by runnin' and shovin' the wagon.

"The wagon twist and turn one of the toms 'round. I guess those toms thought that the other one have 'cided to fight. They give the Gawd-awfullest ruckus you ever did hear.

"Taddie runned up to hold the black tom, while Willie hold the stripe tigah cat. Those was big cats, and hard to hold, 'specially when they have fight in 'em.

"In the tussle to keep them cats from scratchin' each other's eyes out, them boys got scratch on their face and arms. Those cats hiss and hiss at each other and screech and scratch, but those boys hold on.

"Finally, Taddie say, 'Willie, let's make them up. That's what Pa and Ma make us do.' So they hold those toms' snoots right up to each other's snoots, to kiss. But do they kiss? No, it's more scratch, screech, and claw.

"This war just too much, So here those boys come screamin' for Aunt Mariah for help. I throw up my hands in plumb horrah at the sight of those boys. Blood all over their faces and arms, and their clothes torn.

"They screamin,' 'Aunt Mariah, make those blasted toms make up!'

"I took both those torments by the hands and took for the barn. Those cats have broke loose the strings from the wagon and was in a real cat fight, hissin,' spittin,' clawin,' cryin'. The tigah got the best of that fight. That old black tom come up with a clawed-eye. I have to get a buggy whip to sep'rate em.

"Those boys cried 'cause I whip those toms. All through that hullabaloo, that Mammy cat and her little kitten lay in that wagon bed as content as if there have been a cyclone. But cats are the laziest critters on Gawd's green earth, and the dumbest. All they know is to lay 'round in folks' way, to stumble over.

"I got those boys back in the house, wash their dear little dirty-bloody faces and arms. All de Missy ever saw was the torn clothes and scratches. And that was nothin' new for those two boys.

"I swear have she seen them before I clean them, we would have to send for the undataker."

Abe Comes to Billie's Defense

"Mistah Abe loved my Billie's singin,'' Mariah recalled. "I never did know of another kid who could sing a tune clean through like grown-ups, and never miss one single sound like my Billie could when he was only two years old. He could whistle, too, like all the birds, and even get them to fly to him when he was five.

"De Missy say, 'God was good to our Billie.' She have a little spinet. Her would play, but my boy say she couldn' play a horse fiddle. But Gawd bless de Missy, her tried, and I tole her that boy of mine, if he ever hurt that poor woman's feelings, when her war tryin' so hard to help, and tryin' to show as how her like his singin,' I'd plumb wring his haid clean off his shoulders."

Mariah said her husband Henry also liked to sing, and she could sing what suited her. All of their children liked to sing, but Billie was the best.

"Mistah Abe liked sad songs, or the church. 'Specially the colored folks' religion songs. He often laugh, when Billie would sing 'em, though, 'cause Billie clap his hands, roll over on top the ground, and act sometime like he was flyin' to heaven."

Abe asked Billie once, where he learned such "monkey-shines, Bill?" Billie said, "Day ain't monkey-shines, dat's da way dey 'spose be sing. Dat's da way dey all do in church.'

"After that, Mistah Abe would sometimes join in with clappin' and flyin' jestas.

He couldn' sing no more than de Missy could play the spinet. But de Missy say, 'I always know when Mister Lincoln isn't worrying, if there is a time when he isn't, for he goes about singing or whistling.' Sometimes he play the mouf organ. He could do that better than sing."

Mariah described how Billie sang.

"You could never get my Billie to sing soft. He always sing loud and clear. He even wake up in the night and let out such a blast, all the younguns would get stirred up. At last, my Henry lammed him a good one and tole him if he must cut loose, to get outdoors.

"Well, Billie have one hitch at that, singin' out at night when he war eighteen. The white trash 'round here went hog-wild. They have Billie 'rested and he have to go up before Mayor Sutton. [*Goyn Sutton was mayor of Springfield in 1860.*]

"I just 'bout went crazy, 'til Mistah Abe say he see what he could do. My Henry say even if Mistah Abe get him off, them white trash would grab Billie and string him up.

"Well, Mistah Abe war right there that day to stand by Billie. The white trash war there, too. They done have him down for disturb the peace. They say he go out at night and screamed, after they gone to bed and sleep. Say he brayed like a jackass and hooted like a owl.

"Billie was mad as blazes, sayin' such about his singin.' He spoke up and scream, 'Dey's damn liars! I war singin!'

"'Order in the court!' say de mayor.

"Billie say, 'Ah'll show you'ns I can sing, if you'ns let me.'

"Well, Mistah Abe say, 'Bill can sing, your honor. Maybe you will favor me by giving Bill a try. I believe you will be a fine judge of his voice, as you have a marvelous voice and are versed in music. That may be a good way to prove right now, whether he sang or hooted.'

"Mayor Sutton say, 'Request granted!'

"Billie broke loose with all his heart and soul and with all his actin' up. Mayor Sutton and Mistah Abe laugh almost as loud as Billie sing. The white trash done got out of there faster than lightnin', and between Mayor Sutton and Mistah Abe, they say, 'Case dismissed!'

"Billie start to run, too, but that Mayor Sutton call him back and say, 'Not so fast, Billie. You and I need to talk this happening out, as man to man."

"That please Billie a heap, to call him a man.

"The mayor say, 'Billie, you have a fine voice. God has been good to you. You should use it for the glory of God. From now on, don't waste it on anyone who doesn't appreciate it. You really did disturb the peace, but as this is your first offense, I'll let you go if you promise me, you'll not get out at night and wake your neighbors up. When you want to sing, come and sing for me, or go to the Lincoln's, who love your singing and want only the best for you. You may go now.'

"Billie rush out singin' at the top of his voice, 'Glory, glory, halla-lula, ah's on my road to glory now!' He threw his hat in the air and dance and clap every step until he war gone."

Adah Sutton said Mariah told her that a few years later, Billie began singing in both white and black churches until his death in January 1904.

The Last Time Mariah and Billie Saw Abe Lincoln

Because of Henry Vance's fears of hostility against blacks as the United States grew closer to Civil War, he and Mariah moved with their children to Danville, Illinois, near the Indiana border. It was soon after Abraham Lincoln was elected President of the United States on November 6, 1860. Henry got work in the nearby coal mines and Mariah did laundry and house work in the town.

The Union was dissolved on December 20 with the secession of South Carolina. The Lincolns were not scheduled to move to Washington, D.C. until President-elect Abe's inauguration the following March.

Mariah recalled the last time she and Billie saw Abraham Lincoln, a few weeks before Christmas 1860. She said it had been an especially sad parting for Billie and Robert Lincoln because they had become such close boyhood friends.

Mariah told the following to Adah Sutton and I reprint it verbatim from Miss Sutton's manuscript, so quote marks are unnecessary.

Mistah Abe and Mastah Robert come to Danville 'bout Christmas time in 1860. They stop at the Etna House, if I rightly recomemba, for some meeting with some big men in politics and some of their friends.

'Bout noon on that day, a messenga boy bring a note to our home. I tell you I was sure my Henry have been kill or hurt in the mine. But the telegram war from Mistah Abe.

It say on a slip of hotel paper he have send this messenga: "Am at this hotel for a short time today. Robert is with me. I would like for you and Bill to come here between the hours of 3 o'clock and 4 o'clock. We will be very, very disappointed if you don't come. Give messenger your answer. With esteem, A. Lincoln and Robert."

Well, Billie have come in for dinner. He war doin' some home work for the Hegler. They war rich German folks. All those German folks war good to us.

Work or starve, nothing not a soul thing on this earth could have kept my Billie away from getting to see Mastah Robert. When we move here, Mastah Robert was in some school in the East. Maybe Phillips' 'Cademy at Exeter, New Hampshire, or Harvard. So Billie have to come away without a sight of the blessed Mastah Robert.

[Robert Lincoln graduated from Phillips Exeter Academy on September 15, 1859. His first year at Harvard University was 1860-1861, the class of 1864. He was with his father during Christmas vacation.]

We dress in our best clothes. I comb the braids out of my head and made my hair neat, as if it have beeswax on it. Billie slick up, too.

Right at 3 o'clock sharp we reach the steps up to the door of that hotel. Mistah Abe and Mastah Robert almost run down the steps to meet us. I thought Mastah Robert and Billie war goin' to kiss.

Those two Lincolumns war sure pleasured to see us again. Just smilin' and laughin' and shakin' hands. Like no one was on this earth but the Vance's. Just like no white folks was aroun' gapin,' like they have never saw the like before.

Right there and then I know. Pres'dent or no Pres'dent, nothin' war ever change Mistah Abe and Mastah Robert. They would never on this earth ever get the swell head. If bein' Pres'dent wouldn't cause it, nothin' would.

Well, Mastah Robert put his dear arm 'round Billie's shoulda and say, "We'll go into the lobby and visit. We would have come to your home, but Pa has such a short time to get his business settled here, and see those he must see. Pa thought it best to give you the time it would take going to and from your house."

Mistah Abe take me by the arm like I was the Queen of Sheba and help me up those steps. Everyone in that hotel lobby gape. So Mistah Abe take me to each man and a few women there, seated in a kind of circle, and 'troduced me as a very fine colored lady who have lived in the Lincolumm home for ten years. I notice he didn' say servant or wash-woman.

Then Mastah Robert stand up and say, "And this is my best friend, Billie Vance."

Mistah Abe ask 'bout my Henry and our younguns. Said he'd just love to see 'em all, but didn' have the time to do so. I ask him 'bout Willie, Taddie, and de Missy.

He say, "Willie and Taddie coaxed to come along, but Mother, who is the busiest woman this side of Washington, couldn't manage to get them ready, and I suspect she needed them for company."

Sev'ral men come up and shake hands with Mistah Abe. Gratslated him. He could only say a few words to each, 'til he got done visitin' with us. The men what he war there in Danville to see come in.

Some of them have gone out, then come back in like they war anxious for Mistah Abe to be with them. But Mistah Abe war always a poke easy. He tole them men to stay right there, he'd be with them shortly.

Then he say to Billie, "Bill, I have only one desire before I go back to Springfield, and that is to hear you sing again." Then he say to the man behind that desk, "Would you mind if Bill is willing, for him to sing for us? According to my opinion, Bill has one of the most beautiful voices God ever gave to anyone."

He sung da "Mocking Bird Song." ["*Listen to the Mocking Bird.*"] An' he whistle it, too, like da bird, all through dat song when he warn't singin' da words. You couldn' hear a pin drop, as they say. All those folks just couldn' believe it. They was spell boun.'"

Then he knowed Mistah Abe like "*Ah's On Mah Road to Glory Now.*" Before they quit clappin' for the "Mocking Bird," he start singin' the Glory song, makin' all the jesters as he learned in church.

When Billie war done, he quick as a dart sang another song Mistah Abe love. It war a church song. I just cain't recomemba the name, but they all clap, some laugh, an' some cry. Mistah Abe and Mastah Robert, too.

Mistah Abe hole up his'n hand, wipe his'n eyes, and say, kinda perkin' up, "Am I not right when I said Bill has a most beautiful God-given voice? And I know Bill will use it to glorify God."

From that on, Billie war call to sing 'most anywhere.

Mistah Abe give Billie some money. I don't recomemba how much. He give me a basket of fruit and a bag of candy and from his grip what he open, he have toys and presents for all my chillun.

He and Mastah Robert shook our hands, even held our hands, and both them and we cry.

After that meetin,' from that on, I have all da work from da rich and fine folks I could do. Dat war de very last time I see Mistah Abe."

It was not the last time Mariah saw Robert Lincoln. She told Adah Sutton, "Mastah Robert allus come see us'n, when in Danville."

Billie Vance must have known "Listen to the Mocking Bird' was one of Abraham Lincoln's favorite songs. It was based on a poem by Septimus Winner, who also wrote music for it. The song was published in 1856 under the pseudonym "Alice Hawthorne." Winner credited the song's cheerful music to a little African-American boy, Richard Milburn, whom he had heard whistling it.

Mockingbirds are New World birds known for mimicking the songs of other birds and the sounds of insects and amphibians, often loudly and in rapid succession.

The song was very popular during the Civil War, and people danced to it on the White House lawn when news of Confederate General Robert E. Lee's surrender. It continued to be popular throughout the nineteenth century.

The song tells the story of a singer dreaming of his sweetheart, now dead and buried, and a mockingbird whose song they once enjoyed, now singing over her grave. While sad, the melody is moderately lively and was popular to dance to.

"Listen to the Mocking Bird"

I'm dreaming now of Hally,
Sweet Hally, sweet Hally.
I'm dreaming now of Hally
For the thought of her is one that never dies;
She's sleeping in the valley, the valley, the valley
She's sleeping in the valley,
And the mocking bird is singing where she lies.

Listen to the mocking bird,
Listen to the mocking bird,
The mocking bird still singing o'er her grave.
Listen to the mocking bird,
Listen to the mocking bird,
Still singing where the weeping willows wave.

Ah, well I yet remember, remember, remember.
Ah well I yet remember
When we gathered in the cotton side by side.

'Twas in the mild September, September,
    September,
'Twas in the mild September,
And the mocking bird was singing far and wide.

Listen to the mocking bird,
Listen to the mocking bird,
The mocking bird still singing o'er her grave.
Listen to the mocking bird,
Listen to the mocking bird,
Still singing where the weeping willows wave.

Lincoln once said about the song, "It is as sincere as the laughter of a little girl at play." It also may have had personal meaning to him. The "Hally" in the verse may have reminded him of his beloved stepmother, whose pet name was Sally. Or it may have been a hymn to the life he was leaving when he moved to Washington, reminding him of his carefree boyhood days along Knob Creek, Kentucky, where he roamed in the woods barefoot, and of the loss of his loved ones buried there and on other knobs and under other trees.

Death of Willie Lincoln

William Wallace, nicknamed "Willie," was born on December 21, 1850. He became his father's favorite son. Willie and his younger brother Tad were considered to be "notorious hellions" when they lived in Springfield. Abe's law partner, William Herndon, wrote that the boys turned their law office in downtown Springfield "upside-down," pulling books off the shelves while their father appeared oblivious to their behavior."

Willie and Tad both received many presents from strangers while they lived in the White House. Willie was so delighted with a little pony that he road it every day on the grounds of the executive mansion. However, he rode it on cold days as well as warm and one day in early February 1862 he came down with a very bad cold that developed into a fever.

Tad also became ill at the time and with the same symptoms. While Tad recovered, Willie's condition fluctuated from day-to-day. Doctors thought Willie's condition was typhoid fever, which was usually contracted by consumption.

As Willie grew more sick, Mary summoned her seamstress friend and confidante, Elizabeth Keckley, to his bedside. Mrs. Keckley wrote about what happened afterward in her book, *Behind the Scenes*, published in England in 1868, from which I quote:

It was sad to see the poor boy suffer. Always of a delicate constitution, he could not resist the strong inroads of disease. The days dragged wearily by, and he grew weaker and more shadow-like.

He was his mother's favorite child and she doted on him. [*Perhaps because he was the weakest of her sons and needed more love and care*]. It grieved her heart sorely to see him suffer. When able to be about, he was almost constantly by her side. When I would go in her room, almost always I found blue-eyed Willie there, reading from an open book, or curled up in a chair with pencil and paper in hand. He had decidedly a literary taste, and was a studious boy. A short time before his death he wrote this simple little poem:

There was no patriot like Baker,
So noble and so true;
He fell as a soldier on the field,
His face to the sky of blue.

His voice is silent in the hall
Which oft his presence graced;
No more he'll hear the loud acclaim
Which rang from place to place.

No squeamish notions filled his breast,
The Union was his theme;
"*No surrender and no compromise,*"
His day-thought and night's dream.

His Country has *her* part to pay
To'rds those he has left behind;
His widow and his children all,
She must always keep in mind.

Finding that Willie continued to grow worse, Mrs. Lincoln determined to withdraw her cards of invitation and postpone the reception. Mr. Lincoln thought that the cards had better not be withdrawn. At least he advised that the doctor be consulted before any steps were taken.

Accordingly Dr. Stone was called in. He pronounced Willie better, and said that there was every reason for an early recovery. He thought, since the invitations had been issued, it would be best to go on with the reception. Willie, he insisted, was in no immediate danger. Mrs. Lincoln was guided by these counsels, and no postponement was announced.

On the evening of the reception Willie was suddenly taken worse. His mother sat by his bedside a long while, holding his feverish hand in her own, and watching his labored breathing.

The doctor claimed there was no cause for alarm. I arranged Mrs. Lincoln's hair, then assisted her to dress. Her dress was white satin, trimmed with black lace. The trail was very long, and as she swept through the room, Mr. Lincoln was standing with his back to the fire, his hands behind him, and his eyes on the carpet. His face wore a thoughtful, solemn look. The rustling of the satin dress attracted his attention. He looked at it a few moments; then, in his quaint, quiet way remarked—

"Whew! Our cat has a long tail to-night."

Mrs. Lincoln did not reply. The President added:

""Mother, it is my opinion, if some of that tail was nearer the head, it would be in better style;" and he glanced at her bare arms and neck. She had a beautiful neck and arm, and low dresses were becoming to her. She turned away with a look of offended dignity, and presently took the President's arm, and both went downstairs to their guests, leaving me alone with the sick boy.

The reception was a large and brilliant one, and the rich notes of the Marine Band in the apartments below came to the sick-room in soft, subdued murmurs, like the wild, faint sobbing of far-off spirits. Some of the young people had suggested dancing, but Mr. Lincoln met the suggestion with an emphatic veto.

The brilliance of the scene could not dispel the sadness that rested upon the face of Mrs. Lincoln. During the evening she came upstairs several times, and stood by the bedside of the suffering boy. She loved him with a mother's heart, and her anxiety was great.

The night passed slowly; morning came, and Willie was worse. He lingered a few days, and died. God called the beautiful spirit home, and the house of joy was turned into the house of mourning. I was worn out with watching, and was not in the room when Willie died, but was immediately sent for.

I assisted in washing him and dressing him, and then laid him on the bed, when Mr. Lincoln came in. I never saw a man so bowed down with grief. He came to the bed, lifted the cover from the face of his child, gazed at it long and earnestly, murmuring, "My poor boy, he was too good for this earth. God has called him home. I know that he is much better off in heaven, but then we loved him so. It is hard, hard to have him die!"

Great sobs choked his utterance. He buried his head in his hands, and his tall frame was convulsed with emotion. I stood at the foot of the bed, my eyes full of tears, looking at the man in silent, awe-stricken wonder.

His grief unnerved him, and made him a weak, passive child. I did not dream that his rugged nature could be so moved. I shall never forget those solemn moments—genius and greatness weeping over love's idol lost. There is a grandeur as well as a simplicity about the picture that will never fade. With me it is immortal—I really believe that I shall carry it with me across the dark, mysterious river of death.

Mrs. Lincoln's grief was inconsolable. The pale face of her dead boy threw her into convulsions. Around him love's tendrils had been twined, and now that he was dressed for the tomb, it was like tearing the tendrils out of the heart by their roots. Willie, she often said, if spared by Providence, would be the hope and stay of her old age. But Providence had not spared him. The light faded from his eyes, and the death-dew had gathered on his brow.

In one of her paroxysms of grief the President kindly bent over his wife, took her by the arm, and gently led her to the window. With a stately, solemn gesture, he pointed to the lunatic asylum.

"Mother, do you see that large white building on the hill yonder? Try and control your grief, or it will drive you mad, and we may have to send you there."

Mrs. Lincoln was so completely overwhelmed with sorrow that she did not attend the funeral.

[*A severe storm with very heavy rain and strong winds began on the morning of the funeral and continued throughout it, which must have added greatly to Mary Lincoln's distress because thunderstorms terrified her. But she had been too grief-stricken to attend the funeral or burial that afternoon and remained alone in her bedroom, to endure the morning's events as well as the storm as best she could.*]

Willie was laid to rest in the cemetery, and the White House was draped in mourning. Black crape everywhere met the eye, contrasting strangely with the gay and brilliant colors of a few days before. Party dresses were laid aside, and every one who crossed the threshold of the Presidential mansion spoke in subdued tones when they thought of the sweet boy at rest -- "Under the sod and the dew."

Willie's death left deep marks on the Lincoln family. [*Mrs. Lincoln*] was an altered woman... she never crossed the threshold of the Guest's Room in which he died, or the Green Room in which he was embalmed.

Tad changed greatly after his beloved brother's death. While visitors to the White House had earlier called him "exasperating," now they began to say he was "the kindest, brightest, most considerate child" they had ever known.

Now Tad did not play as often with the Taft boys or his other playmates and spent more time being close to his mother and father. He had always slept in the same room with his brother, but now began sleeping with his father. It comforted them both to sleep together.

The bond between them became stronger than ever, as Lincoln also grieved sorely for the loss of his favorite son. On nights when Lincoln stayed up late to work at his desk, rather than go to bed alone, Tad curled up and slept on the floor beside him. Lincoln would gather him up and take him to bed. If Lincoln awoke from a bad dream, he found his little boy sleeping beside him to be a comfort.

The artist Alban Jasper Conrad noticed something different about Lincoln following Willie's death, saying, "ever after there was a new quality in his demeanor -- something approaching awe. I sat in the fifth pew behind him every Sunday [*at services*] in Dr. Guley's church, and I saw him on many occasions, marking he change in him."

John Hay, another White House secretary, wrote that the president "was profoundly moved by his death, through he gave no outward sign of his trouble, but kept about his work the same as ever. His bereaved heart seemed afterwards to pour out his fullness on his youngest child [*Tad*].

On the day President Lincoln was assassinated, he told Mary, "We must both be more cheerful in the future. Between the war and the loss of our darling Willie, we have been very miserable."

Nathaniel Parker Willis, the genial poet, now sleeping in his grave, wrote this beautiful sketch of Willie Lincoln, after the sad death of the bright-eyed boy:

"This little fellow had his acquaintances among his father's friends, and I chanced to be one of them. He never failed to seek me out in the crowd, shake hands, and make some pleasant remark; and this, in a boy of ten years of age, was, to say the least, endearing to a stranger. But he had more than mere affectionateness. His self-possession -- *aplomb*, as the French call it -- was extraordinary.

"I was one day passing the White House, when he was outside with a play-fellow on the sidewalk. Mr. Seward drove in, with Prince Napoleon and two of his suite in the carriage; and, in a mock-heroic way -- terms of intimacy evidently existing between the boy and the Secretary-- the official gentleman took off his hat, and the Napoleon did the same, all making the young President prince a ceremonious salute.

"Not a bit staggered with the homage, Willie drew himself up to his full height, took off his little cap with graceful self-possession, and bowed down formally to the ground, like a little ambassador. They drove past, and he went on unconcernedly with his play: the impromptu readiness and good judgment being clearly a part of his nature. His genial and open expression of countenance was none the less ingenuous and fearless for a certain tincture of fun; and it was in this mingling of qualities that he so faithfully resembled his father.

"With all the splendor that was around this little fellow in his new home, he was so bravely and beautifully *himself*—and that only. A wildflower transplanted from the prairie to the hot-house, he retained his prairie habits, unalterably pure and simple, till he died.

"His leading trait seemed to be a fearless and kindly frankness, willing that everything should be as different as it pleased, but resting unmoved in his own conscious single-heartedness. I found I was studying him irresistibly, as one of the sweet problems of childhood that the world is blessed with in rare places; and the news of his death (I was absent from Washington, on a visit to my own children, at the time) came to me like a knell heard unexpectedly at a merry-making.

"On the day of the funeral I went before the hour, to take a near farewell look at the dear boy; for they had embalmed him to send home to the West—to sleep under the sod of his own valley -- and the coffin-lid was to be closed before the service.

"The family had just taken their leave of him, and the servants and nurses were seeing him for the last time -- and with tears and sobs wholly unrestrained, for he was loved like an idol by every one of them. He lay with eyes closed -- his brown hair parted as we had known it -- pale in the slumber of death; but otherwise unchanged, for he was dressed as if for the evening, and held in one of his hands, crossed upon his breast, a bunch of exquisite flowers—a message coming from his mother, while we were looking upon him, that those flowers might be preserved for her. She was lying sick in her bed, worn out with grief and over-watching.

"The funeral was very touching. Of the entertainments in the East Room the boy had been -- for those who now assembled more especially -- a most life-giving variation. With his bright face, and his apt greetings and replies, he was remembered in every part of that crimson-curtained hall, built only for pleasure -- of all the crowds, each night, certainly the one least likely to be death's first mark. He was his father's favorite. They were intimates -- often seen hand-in-hand.

"And there sat the man, with a burden on his brain at which the world marvels -- bent now with the load at both heart and brain -- staggering under a blow like the taking from him of his child! His men of power sat around him -- McClellan, with a moist eye when he bowed to the prayer, as I could see from where I stood; and Chase and Seward, with their austere features at work; and senators, and ambassadors, and soldiers, all struggling with their tears— great hearts sorrowing with the President as a stricken man and a brother. That God may give him strength for all his burdens is, I am sure, at present the prayer of a nation."

As Willie weakened, his parents spent much of their time at his bedside. Finally, on Wednesday, February 20, 1862, at 5 p.m., he died. Abe said, "My poor boy. He was this earth. God has called him home. I know that he is much better off in heaven, but then we loved him so much. It is hard, hard to have him die."

Willie's death profoundly changed Lincoln. From the testimonies of Mrs. Keckley and the Rev. Phineas D. Gurley, Abe was a broken man, still having to lead a country that was at the same time also experiencing overwhelming losses as casualties in the Civil War mounted every day.

Abe did not return to work for three weeks. He also did not work on any official correspondence for four days. Mary was so overwhelmed by grief that she confined herself to her room in the White House and remained there for three weeks.

She was so distraught that Abe feared for her sanity. Willie's younger brother, Tad, cried for nearly a month because he and Willie had been very close and played so much together, as Mariah Vance remembered. Tad was sick with the same illness at the same time, but survived, only to die nine years later.

A rare bright spot in the Lincoln's life after Willie's death was a visit by the famous circus dwarf, Tom Thumb. He was called "General Tom Thumb," the stage name of Charles Sherwood Stratton (1838-1883) who became famous as a performer of circus leader P. T. Barnum.

On one of his publicity tours, Tom and his wife Lavinia visited the White House and captivated everyone including Tad and his parents. The Thumb's were about the same height. Tom stopped growing when he was 25 inches (64 centimeters) tall and weighed 15 pounds (6.8 kilograms). Apart from this, he was a normal, healthy child and man. His marriage to Lavinia, another dwarf, in 1863 made worldwide headlines. Tom died of a stroke at the age of 45 in 1883. Lavinia died more than 35 years later.

Little is known of their visit to the White House, but Tom Thumb usually sang and danced, joked with a partner, and impersonated famous people such as Cupid and Napoleon Bonaparte. This doubtless entertained Tad and his parents and at least for a day lifted their spirits.

Tad Lincoln

The fourth and youngest son of the Lincolns was Thomas Lincoln, born in Springfield on April 4, 1853. He was named after Abe's father but nicknamed "Taddie" because he had a rather large head and looked like a "wiggly tadpole." Mary Lincoln called him "Taddie," but Abe called him "Tad."

He had dark hair like his father and grew to be tall for his age, also with a lean body. His eyes were called dark or even black.

Tad was born with a cleft lip that left him with a speech impediment. He also likely had a learning disability. These things seemed to endear him to his parents all the more and he was spoiled rotten.

He was said to be an imaginative, responsive, and happy boy but also impatient and quick to become angry and even tearful. The bond between him and his father was described as being strong and tender.

Lincoln's law partner, William Herndon, complained that as boys, Tad and Willie, who were great pals and often got into mischief together, were "little devils." They often played recklessly in the law office, pulling books off the shelves. Lincoln either ignored the boys' antics or encouraged them because he got a good laugh out of them.

In the White House, Abe even let the boys take their ponies and goats inside and ride or play with them.

Also, in Washington, Tad went along with his father to the telegraphic office. Once, while Lincoln was reading some Civil War dispatches, Tad went into another room and drew with black ink all over a white marble tabletop.

The telegraph operator, Madison Buell, scolded Tad and dragged him by the collar into the room where Lincoln was reading. Buell was outraged and said Tad had ruined the table.

Tad may have inherited his father's famous penchant for honesty. He held up his black fingers to admit he had been the guilty party, but said he was just having some fun.

Lincoln's reaction was to take Tad in his arms and tell him, "Come, Tad. Buell is abusing you."

Abe had low tolerance for anyone who reprimanded his boys.

When Willie was ten years old and Tad almost eight and they were living in the White House, they often pulled pranks. Their playmates were often neighbor boys, Holly and Bud Taft. Their older sister Julia sometimes had to look after them.

The Sanitary Commissioner in New York sent Tad a soldier doll which Tad named Jack. The doll was dressed in a Zouave uniform and Tad imagined the toy soldier had been found guilty of sleeping at his post or desertion, and Tad held his own court-martial and sentenced the doll to be shot by firing squad.

Soon after the execution, performed by Tad with a toy rifle, Mrs. Lincoln was in her room when a strange sound came from outside the White House. She learned it was Tad and his pals playing a funeral march at the dead toy soldier's grave as they buried Jack. The boys played the tune using a broken-down fiddle, a dented horn, a paper over a comb, and Tad played his drum.

Mrs. Lincoln asked Julia to go out and not dig among her roses and to stop holding funerals for Jack. The gardener came by with a solution. He suggested to Tad that he get Jack pardoned.

Tad liked the idea. "Come on, Bud," he told his pal. "We'll get Pa to fix up a pardon."

The boys made such a noise outside Abe's inner office that John Hay stopped them. Abe came out asking what was going on, and when Tad told him he wanted Jack to be pardoned, Abe said it was customary to hold a hearing before granting a pardon, and told Tad to state his case.

Tad offered a good defense of Jack and Abe agreed saying that no man shall be twice put in jeopardy for the same offense. He then went to his desk and wrote and signed an official pardon for Jack. It read: The Doll Jack is pardoned by order of the President. A. Lincoln.

The pardon did not last long. A few days later, Tad had Jack found guilty again, this time of being a Confederate spy. He and his pals hanged him from a tree in the garden.

Sometimes. Tad tried to be helpful to his father. One day in 1864, some men had waited a week to see the President. Tad asked about them and they said they were from Kentucky and knew it was the state where his father had been born. He told them to wait and he would ask his father to see them. They were Confederate sympathizers but when Tad asked him to see them and called them his "friends," he agreed.

After granting the Kentuckians a visit, Abe asked Tad why he had called him that, and Tad replied: "Well, I had seen them so often, and they looked so good and sorry, and said they were from Kentucky, that I thought they must be our friends." Abe caressed him with a hand and replied, "That's right, my son. I would have the whole human race your friends and mine, if it were possible."

Lincoln was assassinated just 10 days after Tad's 12th birthday. Robert had gone back to college, so Tad was the only one of her sons that she was living with. She wrote to a friend, "I press the poor little fellow closer, if possible, to my heart, in memory of his sainted father, who loved him so very dearly."

Whereas Willie had been put under the supervision of a tutor, Tad received no primary education at all. He had always been just left to play and enjoy himself, because reading and writing had not been easy for him due to his learning disabilities.

After leaving the White House and moving to Chicago, Illinois, Mary enrolled Tad in a school in Racine, Wisconsin in the autumn of 1865. She wrote a friend that November, "Taddie is learning to be as delighted in his studies as he used to be at play in the White House. He appears to be making up for the great amount of time he lost in W (*Washington*)."

After some time in Wisconsin, Tad was put into a public school in Chicago. He was then 13 but historians doubt he could read and suspected that he had a hard time at school. Fellow classmates taunted and bullied him because of his speech impediment, calling him "Stuttering Tad."

Mary took Tad with her on a sea voyage to Germany in October 1868. Tad got some schooling or tutoring there and Mary wrote in March of 1870, "Taddie is doubtless greatly improving in his studies."

Mother and son moved to England in October of that year. Tad was with a tutor for seven hours a day.

Mary became ill early in the following year, and Tad also showed signs of being sick. They returned by ship to Chicago and Mary improved but Tad grew weaker, and on July 15, 1871, he died. The next day, The *Chicago Tribune* ran an article about his death. It read, in part:

At 7:30 on yesterday (Saturday) morning Tad Lincoln died at the Clifton House on Wabash Avenue, where he had been staying since his return from Europe. The cause of his death was dropsy of the chest. The first symptoms showed themselves while he was abroad, but it was not until his return, the middle of May, that his condition became alarming. He was convalescent at one time, but he got up one night slightly clad and swooned. This was followed by a relapse, after which he grew steadily worse.

Tad was just 18 years old when he died. Mary then began a steady emotional and mental decline. Except for Robert, she was now alone, her other sons having died so young.

While his mother and father had gone to see the play at Ford's theater the night of Abe's assassination, Tad had gone to another theater to see the play *Aladdin and His Wonderful Lamp*. After it was confirmed that Lincoln had been shot, the theater manager announced the news to the audience. Tad leaped out of his seat screaming, "They killed Papa! They Killed Papa!"

Tad was escorted back to the White House and his mother pleaded that he be taken across the street to the house where he had been taken and put to bed. Mary asked from Abe's bedside, "Bring Tad -- he (*Lincoln*) will speak to Tad. He loves him." But Tad was too frightened and grief-stricken so he was put to bed in his own bedroom by a White House doorman. He learned the next morning that his father had died.

Afterward, Tad said, "Pa is dead. I can hardly believe that I shall never see him again. I must learn to take care of myself now. Yes, Pa is dead, and I am only Tad Lincoln now, little Tad, like other little boys. I am not a President's son now. I won't have many presents anymore. Well, I will try and be a good boy, and will hope to go someday to Pa and brother Willie, in Heaven."

Mary, Robert, and Tad then lived together in Chicago. After only a short time, Robert moved out and Tad began attending school there. In 1868 Mary and Tad left Chicago and lived in Europe for almost three years, in Germany and later in England.

They returned then to Chicago where Tad became ill from what doctors said was tuberculosis and probably was a complication of pneumonia and heart failure. He died at the Clifton House on July 15, 1871 at the age of 18.

Funeral services were held at Robert Lincoln's home in Chicago and Tad's body was taken by train to near Springfield where it was buried in the Lincoln tomb at Oak Ridge Cemetery. Robert accompanied Tad's casket on the train, but Mary Lincoln was too distraught to make the trip, remaining in her bedroom in Chicago.

Robert Lincoln, her firstborn and eldest, was now Mary Lincoln's only son living and the only son to survive the death of her husband, Abraham Lincoln.

Robert Visits Mariah

Robert Lincoln frequently visited Mariah Vance at her home in Danville when he was a grown man.

On one occasion, according to Adah Sutton, Robert was enroute from the East to visit his mother in Springfield in 1877 and changed trains to see Mariah in Danville. With him was his little daughter, Mary, and he brought a photograph of his son Abraham whose nickname was "Jack."

A tribute to Robert Lincoln appeared in the August 14, 1926 issue of the *Literary Digest* magazine which states that he knew Mariah Vance and visited her on several occasions at her home in Danville.

The article says that while in Danville to give a rare political speech, he went missing for a few hours before he was to talk in the city park and was found at Mariah's home. He was at her kitchen table where he was enjoying one of his favorite meals she had often prepared for him when she was the Lincoln's cook and housekeeper in Springfield. It was a plate of corn pone and bacon.

Quoting the article: "Mrs. Vance had been cook before the war in the Lincoln household at Springfield and nurse part of the time to Robert Lincoln. Lincoln had heard that the woman was living there and hunted her up. They had spent several hours together. We hustled him away and to the park, where an impatient crowd awaited him.

"No sooner was his talk finished than Lincoln returned to the Vance home, humble as it was, until it was near time for his train. From that day until her death, 'Mammy' Vance received a substantial check each month from [*Robert Lincoln in*] Chicago."

Mariah told Robert that her husband Henry had died in 1865 at the end of the Civil War, so he died a free man. Robert doubtless asked about Billie and learned that his boyhood friend had died on January 16, 1904 at the young age of 39. Nothing is known of Billie's life from the time his parents and siblings left Springfield.

Ruth Painter Randall writes about Robert Lincoln's visit to Mariah Vance in Danville in her book *Lincoln's Sons*, but says it happened in 1900, not 1877. Mariah may have gotten the date wrong, but details of the visit are virtually the same as Ms. Randall wrote. She then added: "They had had a fine time visiting and though he had to leave to make his speech, he returned after it and stayed with her until time to catch his train.

"The aged servant undoubtedly found him a most sympathetic, approachable, and entertaining visitor and from that time on she received a substantial check from him every month. Robert was quietly generous to many who were in need."

This was the only mention of Mariah Vance that Ms. Randall made in her book because she had not known of her or her memoirs.

Abe Lincoln, Children and Pets

It was widely know that Abe Lincoln loved pets and children, not only his own boys but neighbourhood children he knew in Springfield. He did not get to know many children in his White House as President, except the sons and daughters of those who brought them on visits.

Abe Lincoln very considerate of people's feelings, but was even more considerate of children and animals. Although he played a few innocent tricks on animals as a boy, he quickly outgrew any desire to hurt or hunt wild animals for food or trophy.

Lincoln's stepmother testified that "He loved animals" and "he loved children…very well." Even insects elicited his compassion. While his parents went to church, young Lincoln preached his own sermons to his step-family: "Abe preached against cruelty to animals, contending that an ant's life was to it, as sweet as ours."

Lincoln at times went to great trouble to rescue animals who were in any danger. Once, he rescued a pig stuck in the mud because he couldn't bear the thought of its suffering.

His friend Joshua F. Speed recalled a trip he took with Lincoln in 1839 on the way back to Springfield: "We were riding along a country road, two and two together, some distance apart, Lincoln and John. J. Hardin being behind. (*Hardin was afterward made Colonel and was killed in the Civil war at Buena Vista*).

"We were passing through a thicket of wild plum and crab-apple trees, where we stopped to water our horses. After waiting some time, Hardin came up and we asked him where Lincoln was. 'Oh,' said he, 'when I saw him last' (there had been a severe wind storm), 'he had caught two little birds in his hand, which the wind had blown from their nest, and he was hunting for the nest.'

Hardin left him before he found it. He finally found the nest and placed the birds, to use his own words, 'in the home provided for them by their mother.'

"When he came up with the party they laughed at him. Said he, earnestly, 'I could not have slept tonight if I had not given those two little birds to their mother.'"

Illinois politician William Pitt Kellogg recalled: "Next to his political sagacity [*the ability of foresight, discernment, keen perception, able to make good judgments*], his broad humanitarianism was one of his most striking characteristics. He fairly overflowed with human kindness."

Historian Charles B. Strozier noted that "Lincoln's lifelong sympathy for animals was hardly the norm for the frontier."

Another historian, Douglas L. Wilson, said that Lincoln "was unusually tender-hearted. We see this in several reports of his childhood that depict him as concerned about cruelty to animals. When his playmates would turn helpless terrapins on their backs and torture them, which was apparently a favorite pastime, the young future president would protest against it. He wrote an essay on the subject as a school exercise that was remembered years afterward.

"This instinctive sympathetic reaction seems to have been recognized by his stepbrother as a vulnerable spot in Lincoln's makeup, for he is reported as having taunted Lincoln as he was preaching a mock sermon by bashing a terrapin against a tree."

The Lincoln household was a home for the lost and neglected. Cynthia Owen Philip wrote about an incident in which a dog named Jet adopted the Lincoln family: "In mid-October 1861, during the bleak months after the

Union defeat at Bull Run, President and Mrs. Lincoln were driven across the Potomac River to Alexandria, Virginia, to present flags to newly-formed volunteer regiments assembled there.

"On their return to the capital, a sleek black hunting dog trailed their carriage all the way to the White House, trotted after the President right through the front door, and to the delight of the Lincoln children, quickly made himself at home.

"Unfortunately for the boys, the dog had abandoned his owner, army surgeon George Suckley. He read about the new White House resident in a newspaper and went to the White House to claim him. He and Lincoln agreed that Dr. Suckley would furnish one of Jet's pups in exchange for return of his father. But by the time the exchange was to be made in December, Jet had again disappeared, so Dr. Suckley withheld the puppy."

In the White House, Jet took Fido's place. Nurse Rebecca Pomroy reported that "his little dog, Jet, helped relieve Lincoln of "some portion of the burden, for the little fellow was never absent from the Presidential lunch. He was always in Mr. Lincoln's lap to claim his portion first, and was caressed and petted by him through the whole meal.'"

Lincoln had a particular weakness for kittens. One friend from his New Salem days recalled that he "would take one and turn it on its back and talk to it for half an hour at a time."

Another New Salem resident recalled young Abe Lincoln playing with the Carman family kittens, Jane and Susan: "He would take them up in his lap and play with them and hold their heads together and say Jane had a better countenance than Susan had."

Secretary of State William H. Seward presented the Lincoln household with two kittens early in his administration. The August 1861 gifts apparently were a source of comfort for the President. Treasury official Maunsell B. Field wrote: "Mr. Lincoln possessed extraordinary kindness of heart when his feelings could be reached. He was fond of dumb animals, especially cats. I have seen him fondle one for an hour. Helplessness and suffering touched him when they appealed directly to his senses, or when you could penetrate through his intelligence to them."

Mary Lincoln did not share Abe's indulgence of pets and people. When he fed a cat named "Tabby" seated next to him at a White House dinner, she asked him: "Don't you think it's shameful to feed Tabby with a gold fork?" Lincoln replied: "If the gold fork was good enough for former President James Buchanan, I think it is good enough for Tabby."

As President, Lincoln continued to conduct animal rescue missions. Lewis Stanton, son of Secretary of War Edwin M. Stanton, recalled how his father and Lincoln handled one difficult situation at the Soldiers Home in northeast Washington. Lincoln liked to relax there with his son Tad and Stanton's children.

Twenty-five of the one hundred men there had been a company selected to act as Lincoln's mounted escort on his rides to and from the Soldiers Home, where he spent the hot months of the summer.

Lewis Stanton said: "Mr. Lincoln and my father arrived at the cottage. They at once noticed peacocks who were roosting in a small cluster of cedar trees with the ropes and sticks caught in the many small branches and recognized the dangerous and uncomfortable position when on the morrow they would attempt to fly to earth.

"The two men immediately went to work, solemnly going to and fro unwinding the ropes and getting them in straight lines and carefully placing the small pieces of wood where without catching they would slide off when in the morning the birds flew down."

In Springfield, Lincoln's horse "Old Bob" was a valued member of the family. Neighbor Fred T. Dubois recalled: "Old Bob was the family horse of the Lincoln's, which used to draw the family carriage, which had two seats, an open one in front and the rest of the carriage closed. Some of the family always did the driving, as Mr. Lincoln never had a coachman. He had only one man around his house who took care of the horse, etc. Salaries were very meagre at that time, and this man-of-all-jobs wore plain clothes all the time and, as was quite customary in those days, was treated as an equal by everyone."

At President Lincoln's funeral in Springfield Old Bob played an honored role. He was led by the Rev. Harry Brown, an African-American minister who had been an occasional handyman for the Lincoln's.

Children as well as kittens attracted Lincoln's kindness. Dr. Preston H. Bailhache recalled: "Mr. Lincoln was always very solicitous when his boys were sick, and a more devoted father I have never known. His sympathy was almost motherly, and his patience with the children, whether sick or well, opened my eyes to another phase in his wonderful character."

Lincoln's sister-in-law Frances Wallace remembered that he "was the most tender-hearted man I ever knew. I have seen him carry Tad half-way to the office, when Tad was a big boy. And I said to him once: 'Why, Mr. Lincoln, put down that great big boy. He's big enough to walk.'

And he said: 'Oh, don't you think his little feet get too tired?'"

"Mr. Lincoln was fond of children. He took notice of boys, remembered them and spoke to them by name," recalled James S. Ewing of his boyhood in Bloomington, Indiana. Lincoln could have been there on his circuit riding law practice rounds.

"My father was a Democrat. He nicknamed one of my brothers 'Democrat' and he went by that name for years. Mr. Lincoln was a Whig; one day he commented on the nickname 'Democrat.' He said to my other brother, the one next to me, 'I'll call you Whig.' That was Judge W. G. Ewing of Chicago He never has gotten rid of the name Mr. Lincoln bestowed upon him. He has always been called by his friends, 'Whig Ewing,' instead of William Ewing. I only mention this to show the attention Mr. Lincoln paid to boys, even to the extent of knowing their names. Although Mr. Lincoln and my father differed in politics, they were great friends."

Boys and girls in Springfield reportedly adored Mr. Lincoln, for his sense of fun and attentiveness. Philip Wheelock Ayres' grandparents lived across the street from the Lincoln's in Springfield. "My mother recalls the frequent picture of Mr. Lincoln going down the street, wearing his customary tall hat and gray shawl, leading by the hands both Willie and Tad, who were usually dancing and pulling him along. Always his thoughtful face was bent forward, as if thinking out some deep problem, yet he was responsive to the questions of the children. He often brought Tad home on his shoulders."

Illinois State Superintendent of Instruction Norman Bateman recalled of Lincoln: "His surviving friends in Springfield will never forget the long-familiar spectacle of his towering form in the street with Rob or Will or Tad, or all three, perhaps, at his side; nor his exhaustless imperturbability and good-humored patience at the pranks and antics of his boys.

"They would sometimes be sent to hasten his steps homeward to dinner or tea. Promptly sallying forth from his office, he was sure to be stopped by some friend or neighbor at nearly every street corner, for a little chat -- for somehow, the very streets seemed brighter when Abraham Lincoln appeared in them, and the moodiest face lightened up as his gaunt figure and pleasant face were seem approaching. But these detentions were not appreciated by the [Lincoln] boys, whose keen appetites stirred them on to get Paterfamilias home as soon as possible.

"In the course of these efforts by the youngsters, the future President of the United States was very often placed in very amusing positions and attitudes. The spectacle of two little chaps tugging and pulling at his coat-tails, while the third pushed in front, was often beheld -- while Mr. Lincoln, talking and laughing, and pretending to scold, but all the while backing under the steady pressure of the above-mentioned forces, raised his voice louder and louder as he receded, till it died away in the distance and further conversation became impossible. He then faced about, and the little fellows hurried him off in triumph towards home."

Children also adored Mr. Lincoln for his generosity. Illinois State Auditor Jesse K. Dubois lived down the street from the Lincoln's; his son was named for the family's neighbor. Another young neighbor in Springfield recalled an incident with Dubois's son on a "hot summer afternoon in 1858 or 1859. Link Dubois and I were standing on the sidewalk in front of my father's house trying to devise some way to obtain money with which to buy watermelons or ice cream. Link (*who was always resourceful*) suddenly exclaimed: 'Did Mrs. Lincoln ever pay you that money?' (Link knew that Mrs. Lincoln had promised to pay me fifty cents some time before and that I could never muster the courage to ask her for it.) I replied in the negative.

"Said he: 'There comes Old Abe now, you dun him; he'll pay you.' On looking up, I discovered Mr. Lincoln coming east on Market Street, going home. I remember that it required an extra prod from Link. Then I started forward and met Mr. Lincoln at Eighth and Capitol Avenue. I at once proceeded to lay my case before him. He immediately shoved his hand into his trousers pocket and produced a handful of silver coin. Handing me a twenty-five cent piece saying, 'Here is a quarter for the Myers errand.' then another quarter saying, 'This is for the horse you took to Dr. Wallace,' and then another quarter, saying, 'This is for the interest on your money, seventy-five cents in all.' Becoming suddenly rich again we were likewise happy."

Lincoln is said to have had a special way with young people. Decades later, Edward Jonas recalled: "I saw Mr. Lincoln in my father's home in Quincy (*Illinois*) during the great Douglas-Lincoln Debates and during the same period, my father, who was taking part in the campaign, took me with him to various points where Mr. Lincoln was present. I was only thirteen years old and it was, I think, at August or Newcomb, Illinois.

"While my father was speaking, I, with a boy's curiosity, was strolling about the speakers' platform on a tour of investigation when I suddenly felt a tickling behind my ear. Thinking it a bug or fly, I slapped vigorously, but upon its being repeated several times, I became suspicious and turned suddenly and caught the fly. It was Mr. Lincoln with a straw in his hand.

"He made it all right at once by catching me up with his long arm, drawing me to his side and talking to me very entertainingly until his turn came to address the assemblage."

"It seems to me, Robert," (*Lincoln said to him*) that I ought to know you; but, then, you never know about boys of your age, who change every year, and grow out of your knowledge.' "I replied: Mr. Lincoln, I know who you are very well. My father knew you when we lived in Springfield, when he helped to finish the south front and the top work of the Capitol building."

Jonas recalled: "It became a perpetual pleasure. It was an open, cheerful, good-willed friendship, that was never cramped nor stained. I was intimate with him in this office intercourse something over three years, and had a continued friendly relation that was never broken or impaired up to 1860."

Jane Grey Swisshelm, a well-known abolitionist, feminist, and Lincoln critic attended a mass Union meeting at the Capitol on March 31, 1863. She wrote a report on the President for the *St. Cloud Democrat*: "He is very tall and very pale. He walked quickly forward, bowed and took his seat. He was dressed in a plain suit of black which had a worn look; and I could see no sign of a watch chain, white bosom. or color. But all men have some vanity, and during the evening I noticed he wore on his breast an immense jewel, the value of which I can form no estimate.

"This [*jewel*] was the head [*likeness*] of a little fellow, Tad Lincoln, about seven years old, who came with him and for a while sat quietly beside him in one of the great chairs, but who soon grew restless and weary under the long drawn out speeches of the men in the desk, and who would [*wander*] from one member of the Cabinet to another, leaning on and whispering to him, no doubt asking when that man was going to quit speaking and let them go home; and then would come back to father, come around, whisper in his ear, then climb on his knee and nestle his head down on his bosom.

"As the long bony hand spread out over the dark hair, and the thin face above rested the sharp chin upon it, it was a pleasant sight. The head of a great and powerful nation, without a badge of distinction, sitting quietly in the audience getting bored or applauding like the rest of us; soothing with loving care the little restless creature so much dearer than all the power he wields – a power greater than that exercised by any other human being on earth."

The President's love of children was seldom suppressed – even at presidential receptions. "Come here, sister. I can't let you pass me in that way," presidential aide William O. Stoddard recalled the President telling one girl who accompanied her parents to the White House. "Sunny curls, blue eyes, cheeks delicately rosy, a child of seven or eight, warmly but plainly dressed, and now she is trembling with shyness and pleasure as he draws her to him for a kiss and to pat her golden hair. All children are favorites of his, and as she is released his arm goes out again and he has made another capture, but not without a vigorous kicking, and a short, half-frightened squall.

"Up, up, goes a chubby boy of four, and the squall changes to a boyish laugh, for he is a brave little fellow, and he knows a game of toss, even if it lifts him uncommonly high in the air."

Francis P. Blair III recalled that President Lincoln visited the Blair family estate in Silver Springs, Florida, when he was a child: "He drove out to the place quite frequently. We boys, for hours at a time, played 'town ball' on the vast lawn, and Mr. Lincoln would join ardently in the sport. I remember vividly how he ran with the children; how long were his strides, and how far his coat tails stuck out behind, and how we tried to hit him with the ball, as he ran the bases. He entered into the spirit of the play as completely as any of us, and we invariably hailed his coming with delight."

Teenage soldiers found a soft spot in the President's heart. Historian Richard N. Current wrote: "One winter night an Indiana congressman, Schuyler Colfax, left his business at the Capitol and went to the White House to plead for the son of one of his constituents. The boy, convicted of desertion, had been sentenced to die before a firing squad at Davenport Barracks, Iowa, Colfax told the story to President Lincoln, who listened patiently, the replied: 'Some of my generals complain that I impair discipline by my frequent pardons and reprieves; but it rests me, after a day's hard work, that I can find some excuse for saving some poor fellow's life, and I shall go to bed happy tonight as I think how joyous the signing of this name will make himself, his family and friends.'"

Lincoln had a special weakness for children handling adult tasks. Lincoln scholar Kenneth A. Bernard wrote: "When a little girl, in her best dress, arrived at the White House at 7 A.M. and finally saw the President sometime after ten to tell him that her father, who had lost a leg at Fredericksburg, and was now employed at a desk job in the Commissary Department, was going to lose his job because of the jealousy of certain officers, Lincoln told her it would be all right, he would attend to it – and he did."

Union Army chaplain John Eaton wrote of a White House reception "The stream of visitors passed by. In the front line of those who surrounded the open space before the President, waiting their turn, was a little lad who evidently hesitated to approach him, but the kindly motion of Mr. Lincoln's hand brought the child at once to the good man's side. The President bent his great height, and the little boy confided to him his request. I did not hear what was said, – so confidential was the interview between the small boy and the President, – but there was no doubt he had got what he wanted, for he ran off presently with no attempt to disguise his delight."

When a friend from Bloomington, Illinois, was killed in battle in December 1862, President Lincoln wrote a tender letter to the deceased's daughter, Fanny McCullough: "It is with deep grief that I learn of the death of your kind and brave father; and, especially, that it is affecting your young heart beyond what is common in such cases. In this sad world of ours, sorrow comes to all; and, to the young, it comes with bitterest agony, because it takes them unawares. The older have learned to ever expect it. I am anxious to afford some alleviation of your present distress. Perfect relief is not possible, except with time. You can not now realize that you will ever feel better. Is not this so? And yet it is a mistake.

"You are sure to be happy again. To know this, which is certainly true, will make you some less miserable now. I have had experience enough to know what I say; and you need only to believe it, to feel better at once. The memory of your dear Father, instead of an agony, will yet be a sad sweet feeling in your heart, of a purer, and holier sort than you have known before."

President Lincoln was also sympathetic to the wives and children of black soldiers. Nancy Bushrod, a black contraband in Washington, was left with hungry children when her husband's military pay ceased to arrive by mail. She decided to take her case to the President himself and walked five miles to the White House.

After assuring her that he would sign orders the next day for her, President Lincoln called her back as she was leaving the room:

"My good woman, perhaps you'll see many a day when all the food in the house is a single loaf of bread. Even so, give every child a slice, and send your children off to school."

President Lincoln took time to correspond with some youthful gift-givers. In March 1864, he wrote Misses Clara and Julia Brown: "The Afgan you sent is received, and gratefully accepted. I especially like my little friends; and although you have never seen me, I am glad you remember me for the country's sake, and even more, that you remember, and try to help, the poor soldiers."

A very sad event happened in the White House stables on the night of February 10, 1864. Tad was not present to see it, but the stables caught fire and burned to the ground. He heard the bells of fire trucks that rushed to the scene, but later learned that the horses and his and Willie's ponies both had perished in the flames. So, too, did the family's pet goats. When he learned of it, Tad threw himself on the floor and could not be comforted as he cried. The ponies and goats were later replaced.

Near to the end of the Civil War, the Lincoln's had been invited to visit General Grant's headquarters at City

Point, Virginia. The visit was late in March of 1865, about three weeks before the President's assassination.

During this visit, Abe happened to be in the telegraph hut on the day that Grant's army began the final advance of the Civil War. Abe saw three kittens in the hut who appeared to be lost or abandoned, wandering around and meowing. He picked up one the kittens asked it, "Where is your mother?" A soldier nearby said, "The mother is dead."

Abe kept petting the kitten and said, "Then she can't grieve as many a poor mother is grieving for a son lost in battle."

He kept holding the crying kitten while picking up the other two and sat down, holding all three in his lap. He stroked their fur and softly told them, "Kitties, thank God you are cats, and can't understand this terrible strife that is going on. Poor little creatures, don't cry, you'll be taken good care of."

He then looked at Colonel Bowers of Grant's staff and said, "Colonel, I hope you will see that these poor little motherless waifs are given plenty of milk and treated kindly." Bowers promised that he would tell the camp cook to take good care of them.

Ghosts and Spirits of Abe and "Willie"

Many people including Presidents, First Ladies, their children, and famous visitors from other countries have claimed they saw the ghosts of both Abraham Lincoln and his son Willie, or strongly felt their presence, in the White House and at other locations associated with them. Most of those who visited the executive mansion who claimed they saw ghosts of the Lincolns say they were of Abe, while a few said they saw the ghost of his son Willie who died there at the age of 11 on February 20, 1862, just eight days after his father's birthday. The spirits of Abe and Willie reportedly have been seen walking the halls on more than one occasion.

Many people including Mary Todd Lincoln and her sons were Christians, members of the Presbyterian Church. Abraham Lincoln reportedly believed in God but had not been baptized. Many blacks in Lincoln's time were Christians, members of Baptist and other churches. Abe's parents had been members of the Little Mount Baptist Church in Kentucky. His older sister, Sarah, joined the Pigeon Creek Baptist Church when the family moved to Indians.

Biographers say Abe never joined any organized religion, but frequently communed with his Maker in nature, on the long walks he often took in the woods. He read *The Bible* and knew it so well, he could quote from it and often did in his talk to juries, in political campaigns, and in his speeches and letters.

Mary said, about Abe's religious feelings, "He never joined a church, but still he was a religious man. But it was a kind of poetry in his nature, and he never was a technical Christian."

Abe sometimes joined Mary in attending revival meetings held by the Presbyterian Church, but when asked to join the church, he said he "couldn't quite see it."

Typical of many Christians and churchgoers in he 1800s, the Lincoln's also were at times drawn to other spiritual influences. Like his father, Abe believed in dreams that foretold events to come. He often tried to understand what influences his dreams might have on his future. Mary believed in signs and told Abe about their portents of coming events in their lives.

Mary Edwards Brown, granddaughter of Mary Lincoln's sister Elizabeth, Mrs. Ninian Edwards, said in a 1959 interview, "The night before their boy Eddie died, Lincoln had the same dream he always had when something unusual was going to happen – you know, about a ship sailing along fast, that he had the night before he was assassinated."

Lincoln sometimes had premonitions of his death. His friend and biographer, Ward Hill Lamon, said that three days before his assassination, Lincoln told him and others about a dream he had, saying:

"About ten days ago, I retired very late. I had been up waiting for important dispatches from the front. I could not have been long in bed when I fell into a slumber, for I was weary. Soon I began to dream. There was a death-like stillness about me. I heard subdued sobs, as if a number of people were weeping. I thought left my bed and wandered downstairs. There the silence was broken by the same pitiful sobbing, but the mourners were invisible. I went from room to room; no living person was in sigh, but the same mournful sounds of distress met me as I passed along. I saw light in all the rooms; every object was familiar to me; but where were all the people who were grieving as if their hearts would break?

"I was puzzled and alarmed. What could be the meaning of all this? Determined to find the cause of a state of things so mysterious and so shocking, I kept on until I arrived at the East Room, which I entered. There I met with a sickening surprise. Before me was a catafalque on which rested a corpse wrapped in funeral vestments. Around it were stationed soldiers who were acting as guards; and there was a throng of people, gazing mournfully upon the corpse, whose face was covered, others weeping pitifully.

"'Who is dead in the White House?' I demanded of one of the soldiers. 'The President,' was his answer; 'he was killed by an assassin.' Then came a loud burst of grief from the crowd, which woke me from my dream. I slept no more that night; and although it was only a dream, I have been strangely annoyed by it ever since."

On the day of his assassination, Lincoln told his bodyguard, William H. Crook, that he had been having dreams of himself being assassinated for three straight nights. Crook tried to persuade him not to attend a performance of the play "Our American Cousin," a comedy at Ford's Theatre that night, or at least allow him to go along as an extra bodyguard, but Lincoln said he had promised his wife they would go.

As Lincoln left for the theater, he turned to Crook and said, "Goodbye, Crook."

According to Crook, this was the first time he had ever said that. Before, Lincoln had always said, "Good night, Crook."

Crook later recalled that "It was the first time that he neglected to say 'Good night" to me, and it was the only time that he ever said 'Goodbye.' I thought of it at that moment and, a few hours later, when the news flashed over Washington that he had been shot, his last words were so burned into my being that they can never be forgotten."

Both Abe and Mary were said to have been superstitious. Before his marriage to Mary, Abe wrote to his friend Joshua Speed, "I was always superstitious. I believe God made me one of the instruments of bringing you and your wife Fanny together, which union I have no doubt he had foredained. Whatever he designs he will do for me yet." He was apparently referring to his possible marriage to Mary Todd. Abe and Mary were later married by an Episcopal clergyman.

Abe apparently placed a great deal of importance on prayer, especially after becoming President. He is credited with having started, in 1861, the regular national observance of Thanksgiving, held annually on the last Thursday in November.

The observance of Thanksgiving had been promoted by Sarah Josepha Hale, editor of a popular women's magazine. She had recommended that an annual day of thanksgiving be established. Her letters to Lincoln on this cause prompted two of his nine proclamations of fasting, prayer, or thanksgiving.

Presidents, First Ladies, White House staff members, and other famous people have reported feeling ghostly presences, including those of Abraham Lincoln and his young son, Willie. They have told of hearing unexplained noises, and even seeing actual apparitions of Abe, even on their way out of the bathtub while staying at the White House at 1600 Pennsylvania avenue in Washington, D.C.

Abraham Lincoln was assassinated in 1865, but some have said that his spirit, and that of his son Willie have lingered on, and not just figuratively. Over the years there have been multiple purported sights of their ghosts, at the White House and at Ford's Theatre where he was fatally shot. Also, at Fort Monroe in Virginia, and at his tomb in Springfield, Illinois.

The most sightings of Lincoln and Willie's ghosts have been in the White House, where Abe lived during the last four years of his life. Before describing the Lincoln ghosts in more depth, ghosts of other Presidents and First Ladies who have appeared there seem to confirm that the famous residence of presidents is, indeed, haunted.

The ghost of Dolley Madison, wife of President James Madison, is said to have appeared often in the Rose Garden, which she planted outside the White House.

There is even reportedly a Demon Cat in the White House basement that is rarely seen, but when it does appear, it is a foretelling of a national disaster. The kitten grows in size and evil the closer one comes to it. A White House guard saw it a week before the stock market crash of 1929 that began the ten-year Great Depression financial disaster of the 1930s. The cat also reportedly was seen before the assassination of President John F. Kennedy in 1963.

Jackie Kennedy, wife of JFK, also reportedly felt the presence of Abe in the White House.

The ghost of Abigail Adams, wife of President Thomas Adams, has been seen hanging laundry in the East Room. Her ghost appeared frequently during the administration of President William Howard Taft from 1909-1913, and again as late as 2002. It is often accompanied by the strong smell of laundry soap.

Mary Lincoln is said to have had several séances in the Green Room of the White House, hoping to communicate with her dead son Willie. Abe, who attended only one and perhaps two of the séances, actually foresaw his own death more than once, including a dream he had shortly before he was assassinated.

Mary reportedly told friends that in the early 1860s that she had heard President Andrew Jackson stomping and swearing through the halls of the presidential residence, the White House. The Rose Room, which had been Jackson's bedchamber before his death in 1845, is believed by some to be one of the most haunted rooms in the White House.

Jackson's ghostly presence also was recoded in the White House correspondence of Harry Truman, the 33rd President of the United States. In June 1945, just two months into his first term as president, Truman wrote to his wife Bess of the spooky goings-on at his new residence.

Truman wrote: "I sit here in this old house and work on foreign affairs, read reports, and work on speeches, all the while listening to the ghosts walk up and down the hallway and even right here in the study. The floors pop and the drapes move back and forth. I can just imagine old Andy [*Jackson*] and Teddy [*Theodore Roosevelt*] having an argument over Franklin [*Roosevelt*]."

Truman's daughter, Margaret Truman Daniel, once wrote that when her father heard noises in the White House, he imagined that at least one other former president, perhaps Andrew Jackson, was roaming the halls. "I'm sure they're here," he said. "I won't lock my doors or bar them if any of them old coots in the pictures want to come out of their frames for a friendly chat."

By far the most frequently reported ghostly sightings in the White House over the years has been the ghosts, or at least the presence, of Abraham and Willie Lincoln. The first person to say she had actually seen Abe's ghost there was Grace Coolidge, wife of President Calvin Coolidge when he was president from 1923 to 1929. According to her, the lanky former president was standing looking out a window of the Oval Office, across the Potomac River to the former Civil War battlefields beyond.

Lady Bird Johnson, wife of President Lyndon Johnson from 1963 to 1969, reportedly felt Lincoln's presence one night while she was watching a television program about his death.

Most notably, sightings of Lincoln's ghost were frequently reported during the long administration of Franklin D. Roosevelt, from 1933 to 1945. He, like Abe, had presided over his country during a great war.
Roosevelt's wife, Eleanor Roosevelt, used the Lincoln bedroom as her study. She said she would feel Lincoln's presence when she worked there late at night.

Franklin Roosevelt's valet ran screaming from the White House after seeing Lincoln's ghost. Eleanor Roosevelt's maid, Mary Eban, reportedly looked into a room in the White House and then fled "terribly wrought up" after seeing Lincoln sitting on a bed, pulling on his boots.

Mrs. Roosevelt also said that FDR's beloved dog, Fala, a black Scottish terrier, would sometimes bark for no reason at what she felt was Lincoln's ghost.

Queen Wilhelmina of The Netherlands reported that during her visit to the White House in 1942, she heard a knock on her bedroom door in the night. When she answered the knock and opened the door, she reportedly saw Abe Lincoln's ghost, wearing his top hat. She fainted dead away.

British Prime Minister Winston Churchill, who visited President Franklin Roosevelt in the White House more than once during World War II (1939-1945), said he was getting out of the bathtub naked after taking his evening bath, began smoking his customary cigar, and ran right into Lincoln, who was leaning on the mantle above the fireplace. They looked at each other in the face, and Churchill was embarrassed being naked. Lincoln's ghost abruptly vanished.

Churchill had been sleeping in what had been Lincoln's bedroom. He told Roosevelt he would never even go into that room again, much less sleep in it. This encounter with Lincoln's ghost was reported in Mark Nesbitt's book, *Civil War Ghost Trails: Stories from America's Most Haunted Battlefields*.

President Dwight D. Eisenhower also reportedly sensed Abe's presence in the White House during his term in office from 1953 to 1961. So did Ike's press secretary, James Hagerty.

Lillian Rogers Park, a seamstress in the White House, said another staff member told her she saw he ghost of Abraham Lincoln in the room he had slept in, the same one in which Churchill said he had seen Abe. The staff member had told her: "That was old Abe, pacing the floor."

Psychics have speculated that Lincoln's spirit remains in the White House to be on hand in times of crisis, as well as for him to complete the difficult work that his untimely death left unfinished.

Clergyman Norman Vincent Peale said he did not actually see Lincoln's ghost himself, but that a well-know actor, whom he declined to name, had told him that he awakened during an overnight stay in the White House to hear Lincoln's high-pitched voice pleading for help. The actor sat up in bed to see "the lanky form of Lincoln prostrate on the floor in prayer, arms outstretched, with fingers digging into the carpet."

President Ronald Reagan reportedly said that his dog Rex, a spaniel, had twice barked frantically in the Lincoln bedroom and then backed out, tail between its legs, and refused to set foot over the threshold. On another evening, while Reagan and his wife Nancy were watching television in their bedroom, Rex stood up on his hind legs, pointed his nose at the ceiling, and began barking at something invisible overhead. To their amazement, the dog walked around the room, barking at the ceiling.

Reagan said, "I started thinking about it. And I began to wonder if the dog was responding to an electrical signal too high-pitched for human ears, perhaps beamed toward the White House by a foreign embassy. I asked my staff to look into it.

"My daughter Maureen and her husband always stay in the Lincoln bedroom when they visit the White House." She said she sometimes had seen Lincoln's ghost as "an aura [*a light*], sometimes red, sometimes orange during nighttime stays in the house, and that her husband, Dennis Revell, old her he also had seen it.

Reagan said, "One night her husband woke up and saw a transparent figure standing at the bedroom window, looking out. Then it turned and disappeared. His wife teased him mercifully about it for a month.

"Then, when they were here recently, she woke up one morning and saw the same figure standing at the window, looking out. She could see the trees outside right through it. Again, it turned and disappeared."

Reagan said when he investigated the ghostly apparitions of Lincoln, he learned that the Lincoln bedroom was not a bedroom when Lincoln was President. It was his Cabinet Room where he had signed the Emancipation Proclamation ending slavery in the United States.

President Gerald Ford's daughter Susan said she sensed Lincoln's presence near the fireplace in Lincoln's bedroom while she lived in the White House during Ford's presidency from 1974 to 1977.

The most recent report of the ghost or presence of Abraham Lincoln in the White House is that Lincoln was seen conferring with President Barak Obama in the Oval Office.

A Lincoln biographer, Doris Kearns Goodwin, writes in her book *Team of Rivals: The Political Genius of Abraham Lincoln*, that the notion of Lincoln's ghost roaming the rooms of his former residence is in some ways ironic. She wrote that years before Abe became President, one of his Illinois neighbors asked him whether he believed in life after death. "I'm afraid there isn't [*any*]," he responded, but then added, "It isn't a pleasant thing to think that when we die, that is the last of us."

It has been earlier said that Lincoln claimed to have some strange, seemingly prophetic dreams. His friend Ward Hill Lamon said that shortly before his assassination, Lincoln dreamed that he had awakened to discover a wailing crowding the East Room. One of them told him they were mourning for the President's murder.

On the night before his death, Abe reportedly dreamed he was in a mysterious boat or ship, sailing toward a dark and indefinite shore. A dramatization of this dream is shown in the 2012 Stephen Spielberg movie, "Lincoln."

Some paranormal investigators believe that such ghostly sightings are "waking dreams." They are just hallucinations that some people experience when they are drifting off into sleep, or when awakening. They say such experiences are relatively common and do not usually involve ghosts of Abraham or Willie Lincoln.

A most unusual ghost mystery about Abe is a photograph of Mary Lincoln with a ghostly hand on her left shoulder. Many believed it was Abe's hand on her shoulder, comforting her in her grief over his death and that of their sons. The photograph was taken by "spirit photographer" William H. Mumler whose photos are now considered to be hoaxes.

Funny Lincoln

This account of the Lincoln's and their sons should not end on a sad or sorrowful note, so this final chapter will tell some of the oddities of his life, the funny things he said and advised, and then some of the funny stories he loved to tell children and his adult friends.

Unusual Facts About Abe

1. He was the only president to have a patent: Lincoln invented a device to free steamboats that ran aground.

2. He practiced law without a degree. Lincoln had only about 18 months of formal schooling.

3. He wanted women to have the vote in 1836. The future president was a suffragette before it became fashionable.

4. He was a big animal lover, but he wouldn't hunt or fish. If he were alive today, Lincoln would be running an animal shelter.

5. He really was a wrestler. Lincoln was documented as taking part in wrestling bouts.

6. He lost in his first bid for a presidential ticket. The unknown Lincoln was an unsuccessful vice presidential candidate in 1856 at the Republican convention.

7. He never belonged to an organized church. Lincoln read the *Bible* daily and attended church services on occasion but he never joined an organized church in his lifetime. He became more religious during his years as president when

he tried to save the Union during the Civil War and his two youngest sons both died.

8. He didn't drink, smoke, or chew. Lincoln was a simple man of tastes, and he never drank anything alcoholic in the White House.

9. He didn't have a middle name.

10. He hated being called Abe. Apparently, he preferred being called by his last name.

11. Lincoln established Thanksgiving as a national holiday.

12. He was the first president born outside of the 13 original states.

13. Lincoln loved to eat oysters.

14. Lincoln's cat ate at the White House dinner table.

15. His dog was named Fido.

16. His cat was named Tabby.

17. His favorite food was fruit.

18. He was also a big fan of chicken casserole.

19. Lincoln was the first president to use the telegraph.

20. He used the telegraph like e-mail to communicate with generals.

21. Lincoln's mother was killed by poisoned milk.

22. Lincoln's life was saved when he was young when a playmate saved him from drowning.

23. Grave robbers were foiled in 1876 when they tried to steal Lincoln's body.

24. He was the first president with a beard.

25. Lincoln argued a case before the Supreme Court in 1849 and lost.

26. Lincoln failed in his first business. When he was 25, he opened a small store in New Salem with a partner. When his partner died, the store failed and Lincoln worked to pay off their debt.

27. Lincoln's shoe size was very large, between 12 and 14.

28. His coffin has been opened five times.

29. Lincoln was estranged from his father and didn't attend his funeral.

30. Lincoln reportedly played the mouth organ.

31. Lincoln served one term in the U.S. House of Representatives.

32. He ran for the U.S. Senate twice and lost.

33. Lincoln won the popular vote in Senate campaign against Stephen Douglas, but lost the election.

34. Lincoln was shot on Good Friday.

35. Lincoln was photographed with John Wilkes Booth, later his assassin, at his second inauguration.

36. There are no direct living descendants of Abraham Lincoln.

37. Booth's brother saved the life of Lincoln's son Robert on a New Jersey train platform.

38. Lincoln was part of séances after his son Willie died in the White House.

39. Lincoln's animals died in a White House stable fire.

40. A would-be assassin shot at Lincoln in 1864 and put a hole in his stovepipe hat.

41. Lincoln was the first president to be assassinated.

42. He was a judge on the circuit court in Illinois.

43. Lincoln defended the son of his most famous wrestling opponent from murder charges.

44. Lincoln battled depression for much of his life.

45. Lincoln was seemingly obsessed with cats.

46. He was set to take part in a duel, but it was cancelled at the last second.

47. Lincoln kept his important documents inside his hat.

48. Lincoln's dog Fido was killed by a drunken assailant a year after Lincoln died.

49. Lincoln's suit was made by Brooks Brothers.

50. Lincoln's guest at Ford's Theatre was Ulysses S. Grant, who cancelled at the last second.

Funny Lincoln quotes

Abraham Lincoln said many humorous things and told many jokes in his lifetime:

- It has been my experience that folks who have no vices have very few virtues.

- When I hear a man preach, I like to see him act as if he were fighting bees.

- If I were two-faced, would I be wearing this one?

- Most people are about as happy as they make up their minds to be.

- Better to remain silent and be thought a fool than to speak out and remove all doubt.

- Whatever you are, be a good one.

- He can compress the most words into the smallest ideas better than any man I ever met.

- When you have got an elephant by the hind leg, and he is trying to run away, it's best to let him run.

- You can fool some of the people all of the time, and all of the people some of the time, but you cannot fool all of the people all of the time.

- Whenever I hear anyone arguing for slavery, I feel a strong impulse to see it tried on him personally.

- If this is coffee, please bring me some tea; if this is tea, please bring me some coffee.

- Labor is prior to, and independent of capital. Capital is only the fruit of labor, and could never have existed if labor had not first existed. Labor is the superior of capital, and deserves much the higher consideration.

- No matter how much cats fight, there always seem to be plenty of kittens.

- Things may come to those who wait, but only the things left by those who hustle.

Many presidents have exhibited senses of humor throughout our nation's history. None, however, is any better known for his wit than was Lincoln. No matter the situation, it always reminded him of a story, and more often than not, the story was amusing.

It would seem that his zest for humor appeared early in life. At the age of 16 or 17 he wrote these two poems:

> **Abraham Lincoln**
> **His hand and pen**
> **He will be good but**
> **God knows when**

and,

> **Abraham Lincoln is my name**
> **And with my pen I wrote the same**
> **I wrote in both hast(e) and speed**
> **And left it here for fools to read.**

Following are some of the favorite stories Lincoln loved to tell to children and adults. Even during his most trying times, he found that humor helped him to survive them. He also told these stories to soldiers in hospitals who were wounded during the Civil war.

Some are considered to be true, but others could have been embellished by others over the years. The stories are all fun to read and it is easy to imagine Abe telling them.

Abe Needs His Hair Combed

President Lincoln had the ability to laugh at himself and he greatly enjoyed telling stories in which he was the object of the joke. He especially liked this one: "When I was nominated at Chicago, I had never before sat for a photograph. One fellow thought that many people might like to see what I looked like, so he immediately bought the negative and began selling photographs of me all over the country. I happened to be in Springfield when I heard a boy selling them on the streets. 'Here's your likeness of "Abe" Lincoln!" he shouted. "He'll look a lot better once he gets his hair combed!'"

Biting Flies

Some of Lincoln's friends once warned him that a particular member of his Cabinet was working behind the President's back in hopes of gathering support for a presidential bid of his own, even though he knew that Lincoln was to be a candidate for re-election. The friends believed that the Cabinet officer should either be called upon to refrain from such underhanded tactics or be removed from office. Lincoln mulled their suggestion over, then used this story to explain why he wouldn't take any action:

"One day my brother and I were plowing. I was driving the horse and my brother was holding onto the plow. The horse was usually lazy, but all of a sudden he ran across the field so fast that even I, with my long legs, had trouble keeping pace with him. When we got to the end of the furrow, I found that an enormous fly had fastened upon him, causing him to bolt. I knocked the fly off. My brother asked me what I did that for, and I told him I didn't want to see the old horse bitten like that. My brother protested, 'that's the only thing that made him go.'

Lincoln gazed at his friends before continuing, "If (*the cabinet officer*) has a Presidential fly biting him, I'm not going to knock it off, if it will only make his department go."

The Problem with the World

One of Lincoln's neighbors told how he went to his door one day to determine why some children in the street were shouting. He saw Lincoln walking past with two young boys in tow. "What's the matter, Mr. Lincoln?" the neighbor asked. "The same thing that's the matter with the whole world," Lincoln answered. "I have three walnuts, and each one of them wants two of them."

Nobody Ever Died in Here!

A man was complaining to the President that a friend of his had been expelled from New Orleans because he was a Union sympathizer. When the man asked to see the writ by which he was expelled, he was summarily told that the Confederate Government would do nothing illegal, and so they had issued no writs. They were simply hoping to make him go of his own free will.

Naturally, that reminded Lincoln of a story, and he remarked that he had known of a hotel keeper in St. Louis who boasted that nobody ever died in his hotel. "Of course," Lincoln said with a twinkle in his eye, "Anytime a guest appeared to be in danger of dying he was carried out to die in the gutter."

Let the Elephant Run

Assistant Secretary of War Charles A. Dana had learned that a man named Jacob Thompson, who had been causing the government many problems, was about to escape to Liverpool. Dana approached Lincoln with the news. Lincoln asked Dana what Secretary of War Edwin Stanton thought about it. Dana answered, "He thinks we should arrest him."

Lincoln replied, "I disagree. If you have an elephant on your hands that wants to run away, you better let him run."

We Need Hardtack

Secretary of War Stanton told the President this story, which Lincoln truly enjoyed. Lincoln particularly enjoyed stories at the expense of those in positions of authority, especially if they had no sense of humor themselves, which pretty well described Stanton.

Stanton had been travelling by boat up the Broad River in North Carolina, and a Federal picket yelled out, "What are you carrying on that tug?" The answer came back, "The Secretary of War and Major General Foster."

The picket replied, "We've got enough Major-Generals here. How about bringing us some hardtack?"

[*Hardtack was a very hard cracker often eaten by soldiers during the Civil War and sailors during long sea journeys. It was an inexpensive and long-lasting biscuit made from flour, water, and sometimes salt.*]

Who Cares Who Started It?

Lincoln was addressing some visitors, and he said, "Some Union supporters oppose any accommodation or yielding to the South in any manner because the Confederates began the war and should be held responsible. Now this reminds me of a good story I heard once, when I lived in Illinois."

"A farmer had a vicious bull that took after anybody who tried to cross the field. One day a neighbor climbed the fence and was soon running for his life. This man was fast, though, and he got to a tree with the bull close behind. There was no time to climb the tree, so he led the bull in a chase around the tree. He finally was able to grab the bull by the tail. The bull was now at a disadvantage. He couldn't catch the man and he couldn't shake him from his tail. The more they ran the madder the bull got. He pawed up the earth and bellowed until you could hear him miles away. Finally, he broke into a dead run, the man still hanging onto his tail.

"The neighbor, now dragging along behind, shouted at the bull, 'Darn you, who commenced this fuss?"

"That's our situation here," summarized Lincoln. "It's our duty to settle this fuss at the earliest possible moment, no matter who commenced it."

Lost Time

Lincoln told the story of a witness in court. When he was asked how old he was he answered, "Sixty." It was apparent that the witness was much older, so he was asked the same question again. His answer was the same.

At that point the judge chastised the witness, saying, "The court knows you to be much older than sixty."

The witness thought quickly, realizing he'd been had, and answered, "You're probably thinking of those ten years I spent in Maryland. That was so much time lost, I don't count it."

The Road to Hell

A friend visited President Lincoln and found him to be in a foul mood. "I'm afraid I have made Senator Wade of Ohio my enemy for life," Lincoln said. "Wade was here just now trying to convince me that I should dismiss Grant, and, in response to something he said, I remarked that that reminded me of a story."

"What did Wade say?" the friend asked.

"He wasn't happy," Lincoln answered. 'Everything with you is story, story, story!' Senator Wade said. He said I was the father of every military blunder that we've made, and that I am on the road to hell and I am not a mile off this minute."

"What did you say to that?" the friend asked.

"I just said to him," the President chuckled, "Senator, that is just about the distance from here to the Capitol, is it not?"

Lincoln's Thoughts on Bragging Generals

Lincoln had a low tolerance for Union generals who exaggerated their accomplishments and bragged about what they would do to the enemy next time they met. One of these very generals had just been badly defeated by the Confederates, and Lincoln related this story to those who were present:

"He (*the general*) reminds me of the fellow who owned a dog which, he claimed, loved to fight wolves. The dog's owner said that his animal spent its entire day tracking down and killing wolves.

"One day a group of the dog-owner's friends organized a hunting party and invited the dog-owner and the dog to go with them. They soon noticed that the dog-owner was not excited about joining them. He said he had a business engagement, which greatly amused the others, who all knew that the man was so lazy that he would never have any reason to have a 'business engagement.' They ridiculed him to a point where he had no choice but to go along.

"The dog, on the other hand, was excited to be going out into the woods, and the hunting party was soon on its way. Wolves were in abundance, and it wasn't long before a pack was discovered. The dog saw the ferocious animals about the same time the wolves spotted him, and the chase was on. The hunting party followed on horseback.

"The wolves and dog soon were out of sight, but the party followed the sounds of the chase. Soon they arrived at a farmhouse, where a farmer stood leaning against his gate.

"'Did you see anything of a wolf-dog and a pack of wolves around here?'" he was asked.

"'Yep,' he replied.

"'How were they going?' came the next question.

"'Purty fast,' he answered.

"'What was their position when you last saw them?'

"'Well,' replied the farmer, 'The dog was a just a little bit ahead.'"

"Now, gentlemen," said the President to his visitors, "that's exactly where you'll find most of these bragging generals when they get into a fight with the enemy."

Pretense

Lincoln found himself in a stifling courtroom one hot summer day, pleading his client's case. The opposing lawyer, in a concession to the oppressive heat, took off his coat and vest as the debate went on. The man's shirt had its buttons in the back, a style which was unusual even then.

Lincoln looked at his opponent and sized up the man's apparel. Knowing that the rural jury disliked pretension of any kind, or any attempt to show superior social rank, he said: "Gentlemen of the jury, having justice on my side, I don't think you will be at all influenced by the gentleman's pretended knowledge of the law, when you see he does not even know which side of his shirt should be in front." The jury burst into laughter, and Lincoln won the case.

If I Lose, I'll Lose Doing the Right Thing

In August, 1864, the nation's morale was low. The war was dragging on and the President had just issued a call for an additional five hundred thousand troops. The Presidential election was just around the corner and many of Lincoln's supporters feared that the call for more men at such a crucial time would injure, if not destroy, Lincoln's chances for re-election. Lincoln's response? "As far as my re-election," he said, "it matters not. We must have the men. If I go down, I intend to go, like the *Cumberland*, with my colors flying!"

(*The Cumberland was a Confederate blockade-runner that sank in Georgia.*)

The Doctor Learns a Lesson

The speaker is Dr. Jerome Walker, of Brooklyn, who was showing President Lincoln through the hospital at City Point.

"Finally, after visiting the wards occupied by our invalid and convalescing soldiers," said Dr. Walker, "'we came to three wards occupied by sick and wounded Southern prisoners. With a feeling of patriotic duty, I said: 'Mr. President, you won't want to go in there; they are only rebels.' "I will never forget how he stopped and gently laid his large hand upon my shoulder and quietly answered, 'You mean Confederates!'" And I have meant Confederates ever since.

"There was nothing left for me to do after the President's remark but to go through these three wards and I could not see but that he was just as kind, his handshakings just as hearty, his interest just as real for the welfare of the men, as when he was among our own soldiers."

Humility

Union General George McClellan showed little respect for Lincoln. As time went on, his contempt for the President became more and more blatant, and he often kept Lincoln waiting while he transacted business with others. This discourtesy was so apparent that even McClellan's staff seemed embarrassed by it, and it often drew comments from newspaper reporters. The President was finally asked about it. Humbly, Lincoln stated that McClellan's disrespect was not a problem with him, if the slow-moving general would just initiate a battle. "I'll even hold McClellan's horse," the President said, "If he will only bring us some success."

Now, That's Ugly!

This story may or may not be true, but it is the type of humor Lincoln loved and is something he easily could have said, if indeed, he didn't.

The story goes that Lincoln was stopped one day by a man who stuck a revolver almost into his face. Under the circumstances Lincoln quickly realized that any resistance was unwise. Trying to remain calm, he inquired, "What seems to be the matter?"

"'Well,' replied the man, 'A long time ago I swore that if I ever came across an uglier man than myself I'd shoot him on the spot."

"Well," supposedly said Lincoln. "Go ahead and shoot me then, because if I am an uglier man than you I don't want to live."

All the Candidates Are Sick!

All presidents are constantly besieged with requests for favors, and at no time are the requests more frequent than when an appointment is to be made. Lincoln was to appoint a Commissioner to the Hawaiian Islands, and eight applicants had filed their papers.

"A delegation made a personal appearance at the White House on behalf of a ninth candidate. The delegation was quick to point out that their man was quite capable, but more importantly, was also in poor health. Sending him to Hawaii, they reasoned, would be of great benefit to his health. Obviously, the President had heard this story before, probably more than once. He did not wish to hear the same story again, and he drew the interview to a close with this remark: "Gentlemen, I am sorry to tell that there are eight other applicants for this position, and I understand that everyone of them is sicker than your man."

What the Wounded Soldiers Thought

Lincoln often visited wounded soldiers in Washington area hospitals. In addition to inquiring about their health he often entertained the patients with his stories. He had just left one such facility when a visitor to the same hospital heard wounded soldiers laughing and talking about the President. The soldiers seemed in such good spirits that the visitor was curious, and he approached the bedside of one of the patients.

"You must be very slightly wounded," he said to open the conversation.

"Yes," the soldier replied, "Very slightly. I have only lost one leg, and I'd be glad to lose the other, if I could hear some more of 'Old Abe's'' stories."

A typical story told during his Presidency reflected on his critics: "A frontiersman lost his way in an uninhabited region on a dark and tempestuous night. The rain fell in torrents, accompanied by terrible thunder and more terrific lightning. To increase his trouble, his horse halted, being exhausted with fatigue and fright. Presently a bolt of lightning struck a neighboring tree, and the crash brought the man to his knees. He was not an expert in prayer, but his appeal was short and to the point: 'Oh, good Lord, if it is all the same to you, give us a little more light, and a little less noise."

The Rev. Phineas Gurley, pastor of the Presbyterian church in Washington where President Lincoln worshiped, recalled being present when a Cabinet member asked President Lincoln what was "the proper manner of telling a story. How is it yours are so interesting?" Mr. Lincoln replied that "there are two ways of relating a story. If you have an auditor who has the time, and is inclined to listen, lengthen it out, pour it out slowly as if from a jug. If you have a poor listener, hasten it, shorten it, shoot it out of a pop-gun."

Illinois railroad engineer Richard Price Morgan recalled a story that Mr. Lincoln told him while the two stayed in a Bloomington rooming house: "Speaking of the relative merits of New England rum and corn juice, as he called it, to illustrate the human mind, he told me this story of John Moore, who resided south of Blooming Grove, and subsequently became State Treasurer: Mr. Moore came to Bloomington one Saturday in a cart drawn by a fine pair of young red steers.

"For some reason he was a little late starting home, and besides his brown jug, he otherwise had a good load on. In passing through the grove that night, one wheel of his cart struck a stump or root and threw the pole out of the ring of the yoke. The steers, finding themselves free, ran away, and left John Moore sound asleep in his cart, where he remained all night.

"Early in the morning he roused himself, and looking over the side of the cart and around in the woods, he said: 'If my name is John Moore, I've lost a pair of steers; if my name ain't John Moore, I've found a cart.' After a good laugh together, Lincoln said: 'Morgan, if you ever tell this story, you must add that Moore told it on himself.'"

Stories and humor changed Mr. Lincoln's looks as well as his mental state. James Grant Wilson, who was later a general in the Civil War, recalled meeting Mr. Lincoln in his law office in 1858. Wilson wrote that "his gray-ish-brown eyes were perhaps the saddest I ever saw. However, when a good story was told, whether by himself or another, his homely face lighted up till he was positively handsome."

A young man who came to Mr. Lincoln's office for legal services reported: "As he rose from his chair he seemed to undouble like a pocket rule, his legs and arms disproportionately long, his hair dishevelled, his clothing seedy, and his general appearance quite unprepossessing. But he had not talked to me ten minutes in his quiet, sympathetic way before I thought him about the handsomest man I had ever seen."

There still was an innate dignity about the man. "Nothing can be more absurd than to picture Lincoln as a combination of buffoon and drummer," recalled Frederick Trevor Hill. " He was frequently the life of our little company, keeping us good-natured, making us see the funny side of things and generally entertaining us; but to create the impression that the circuit was a circus of which Lincoln was the clown is ridiculous."

Lincoln sometimes injected humor into his campaign speeches in the 1830s and 1840s. Friend Philip Clark remember that in Mr. Lincoln's congressional campaign against Peter Cartwright in 1846, Mr. Lincoln "asked Cartwright if General [*Andrew*] Jackson did right in the removal – I believe it was – of the bank deposits. Cartwright evaded the question and gave a very indefinite answer.

Lincoln remarked that Cartwright reminded him of a hunter he once knew who recognized the fact that in summer the deer were red and in winter gray, and at one season therefore a deer might resemble a calf. The hunter had brought down one at long range when it was hard to see the difference, and boasting of his own marksmanship had said: 'I shot at it so as to hit it if it was a deer and miss it if it was a calf.' This convulsed the audience, and carried them with Lincoln."

By the 1850s, Lincoln generally campaigned without such stories. Logic and facts were increasingly central to his political rhetoric. Henry Clay Whitney wrote that "it is a singular fact that Lincoln very rarely told stories in his speeches. In both his forensic and political speeches, he got down to serious business, and threw aside the mask of Momus altogether. I never heard him narrate but one story in a speech, which was this: 'A man on foot, with his clothes in a bundle, coming to a running stream which he must ford, made elaborate preparations by stripping off his garments, adding them to his bundle, and, tying all to the top of a stick, which enabled him to raise the bundle high above his head to keep them dry during the crossing. He fearlessly waded in and carefully made his way across the rippling stream, and found it in a place up to his ankles.'"

Aide John Hay recalled a story which others remembered as well: "One night, when [Ambrose] Burnside was at Knoxville, and [James] Longstreet had gone from Chattanooga to capture or destroy him, a dispatch came from [Union General John Gray] Foster, at Cumberland Gap, saying, 'Scouts just in report hearing firing in the direction of Knoxville.' I took it to the President. He read it, and said, 'That is good.'

"I expressed my surprise at his taking so cheerful a view of Burnside's deadly danger. He said, 'I had a neighbor out West, a Sally Taggart, who had a great many unruly children whom she did not take very good care of. Whenever she heard one squall in some out-of-the-way place, she would say, 'Well, thank Goodness, there's one of my young ones not dead yet! As long as we hear guns, Burnside is not captured.'"

Sad stories were a critical outlet for the perpetually stressed President. Writer Norman Cousins, who himself once laughed his way back from a serious illness, observed: "What seems clear is that the greater the weight of his Presidency, the greater was the need for release. Laughter to him was not merely a random physical response to humor but a physiological reality that was essential for restoration and rejuvenation."

Lincoln enjoyed hearing as well as telling good stories. Noah Brooks recalled: "Anything that savored of the wit and humor of the soldiers was especially welcome to Lincoln. His fondness for good stories is a well-accepted tradition, but any incident that showed that 'the boys' were mirthful and jolly in all their privations seemed to commend itself to him. He used to say that the grim grotesqueness and extravagance of American humor were its most striking characteristics.

"There was a story of a soldier in the Army of Potomac, carried to the rear of battle with both legs shot off, who seeing a pie-woman hovering about, asked, 'Say, old lady, are them pies sewed or pegged?' And there was another one of a soldier at the battle of Chancellorsville, whose regiment, waiting to be called in the fight, was taking coffee. The hero of the story put to his lips a crockery mug which he had carried, with infinite care, through several campaigns. A stray bullet, just missing the coffee-drinker's head, dashed the mug into fragments, and left only its handle on his finger. Turning his face in that direction, the soldier angrily growled, 'Johnny, you can't do that again!' Lincoln, relating these two stories together, said, 'It seems as if neither death nor danger could quench the grim humor of the American soldier.'"

A few days before he died, Lincoln visited Richmond, Virginia. Debris in the James River forced some of the boats to drop out. He said it reminded him of a story about "a fellow [who] once came to ask for an appointment as a minister abroad. Finding he could not get that, he came down to some more modest position. Finally he asked to made a tide-waiter. When he saw he could not get that, he asked for an old pair of trousers. It is well to be humble."

Lincoln himself used stories to poke fun at himself. When he stopped at Columbus on the way to Washington in 1861, President-elect Lincoln remarked: "Two friends of mine in Illinois were talking about me. One said, 'Mr. Lincoln is a self-made man, isn't he?' to which the other said, 'Yes, but I didn't know that he ever took much pains about it.'"

Historian Benjamin Thomas wrote: "Lincoln's humor, in its unrestraint, its unconventionality, its use of back-country vernacular, its willingness to see things as they were, its shrewd comments in homely, earthy phrase, its frequent contentment with externals, typified the American humor of his time. Two strains – pioneer exaggeration and Yankee laconicism – met in him. In his humor, as in his rise from obscurity to fame and in his simple, democratic faith and thought, he epitomized the American ideal."

Scholar Lois Einhorn wrote: "Lincoln's pragmatic attitude toward life and speaking and his need to be understood – to reach the people — help explain the homespun nature of his humor.

Reflecting the Western frontier, his stories were colloquial, concrete, colorful, and occasionally off-color. They included commonplace details, vivid imagery, frontier vernacular, and short, straightforward sentences that sometimes deviated from the formal rules of grammar. The simplicity of his stories made them easier to digest. They usually employed analogical logic and sometimes used the techniques of exaggeration, distortion, and caricature often associated with the 'tall tales' of the West.

Few of his stories were uproariously funny; they sought to make listeners smile while understanding a serious point."

Longtime friend Ward Hill Lamon wrote: "No one knew better than Mr. Lincoln that genuine humor is 'a plaster that heals many a wound;' and certainly no man ever had a larger stock of that healing balm or knew better how to use it. His old friend I. N. Arnold once remarked that Lincoln's laugh had been his 'life-preserver.' Wit, with that illustrious man, was a jewel whose mirth-moving flashes he could no more repress than the diamond can extinguish its own brilliancy. In no sense was he vain of his superb ability as a wit and story-teller."

Epilogue

Abraham Lincoln loved his sons and they loved him, but they and Mary were a family bereft of grief, sorrow, and tragedy. Perhaps their lives were the price to pay for ending slavery in America and reuniting the Union, a process that continues today because of recurring racial divisions.

That reunion may depend on the words of Lincoln himself when he said that everyone should "follow the better angels of their nature." He was a strong believer in neighbor loving neighbor; if not love, at least respecting each other's differences and getting along as Americans.

As Lincoln said to Congress in the closing remarks of his 1st Inaugural address on March 4, 1861, addressing them as "Fellow citizens of the United States":

"In *your* hands, my dissatisfied fellow-countrymen, and not in *mine*, is the momentous issue of civil war. The Government will not assail *you*. You can have no conflict without being yourselves the aggressors. *You* have no oath registered in heaven to destroy the Government, while I shall have the most solemn one to preserve, protect, and defend it.

"I am loath to close. We are not enemies, but friends. We must not be enemies. Though passion may have strained, it must not break out bonds of affection. The mystic chords of memory, stretching from every battlefield and patriot grave to every living heart and hearthstone all over this broad land, will yet swell the chorus of the Union, when again touched, as surely they will be, by the better angels of our nature."

On December 1, 1862, one month before signing the Emancipation Proclamation, Lincoln sent a message to Congress, concluding saying:

"We can succeed only by concert [*working together*]. It is not 'can *any* of us *imagine* better?,' but 'can we *all* do better?' The dogmas of the quiet past are inadequate to the stormy present. The occasion is piled high with difficulty, and we must rise – with the occasion. As our case is new, so we must think anew, and act anew. We must disenthrall ourselves, and then we shall save our country."

Lincoln used the word "disenthrall" to mean we must divest ourselves from time-honored ways of doing thinks, or we will never progress as a society.

It seems fitting to close this book with an elegy for Lincoln by his most famous biographer, Carl Sandberg who wrote the following poem in his memory called *"The Long Shadow of Lincoln: A Litany,"* from *The Complete Poems of Carl Sandberg,* published by Houghton Mifflin Harcourt in 1970. The closing lines recall Lincoln's words:

> *The earth laughs, the sun laughs*
> *over every wise harvest of man,*
> *over man looking toward peace*
> *by the light of the hard old teaching:*
> *We must disenthrall ourselves.*

The closing words are prophetic because racial strife has recently resurfaced in America. Lincoln's words and those of an 1854 African-American spiritual, *"A Balm in Gilead,"* can provide solace and healing, direction and hope, for a new reunion of the nation.

The spiritual is a reference from the *Bible* (Jeremiah chapter 8, v. 22) where "the balm of Gilead" is interpreted to be a spiritual medicine from God that is able to heal Israel, and sinners or those in conflict in general.

There is balm in Gilead,
To make the wounded whole;
There's power enough in heaven,
To cure a sin-sick soul.

Abraham and Mary Lincoln and their sons were personifications of that balm. They were the better angels of America's nature.

CPSIA information can be obtained
at www.ICGtesting.com
Printed in the USA
FSHW022217261120
76361FS